T0129388

COMPLETING THE WHEEL

An Adventure in Creativity and Life

Warren Dittmar

iUniverse, Inc.
New York   Bloomington

Completing the Wheel
An Adventure in Creativity and Life

iUniverse books may be ordered through booksellers or by contacting:

iUniverse
1663 Liberty Drive
Bloomington, IN 47403
www.iuniverse.com
1-800-Authors (1-800-288-4677)

ISBN: 978-1-4401-9651-5 (pbk)
ISBN: 978-1-4502-0165-0 (cloth)
ISBN: 978-1-4401-9652-2 (ebk)

Printed in the United States of America

iUniverse rev. date: 3/2/2010

Contents

The Wheel

Chapter One

When I was six, I took a book of matches from our Bronx apartment to an empty nearby lot and tried to light a fire. I had gathered what I could to ensure a good blaze. After I had tried unsuccessfully several times, striking one match after another, the collected sticks of wood and pieces of cardboard suddenly ignited and brilliant flames danced before me. I was delighted. I had created a fire all by myself! I was more than six. I was ten. I was almost a man. It wasn't until I had difficulty putting it out that I realized that there were limitations caused by my lack of experience and knowledge. Some nearby wood caught fire and what started as a little blaze became a large one that was difficult to control.

Fifty-some years later, the memory of that fire is still vivid and striking. We all have certain memories that somehow override time and remain powerful reminders of our past experiences. But what is the significance of these memories? What allows them to remain poised just beneath the surface of consciousness to spontaneously appear at a moment's reflection? Perhaps it is our longing and search for the story of our lives. Throughout the ages, the imaginative story has been a way for man to give meaning to his experience. I believe that without the imaginative story of our experiences we are, as a wheel with missing spokes, stuck in the muck of our disconcertingly incomplete lives.

It is our imaginative life that keeps our energy up, our hopes alive, and our fires going. Too often we are captured and dulled by our peers or teachers. We are clobbered by some factual or semi factual details and denied our creative rights by one of the ruling dictators. It could be our own childhood experiences that erroneously proclaim our lack of creativity, perhaps even at the hands of one of our parents, in a meaningful way, even a suggestion that creative expression is not richly rewarded and of little value can foster a hesitation—if not an all-out rejection of its possession. It is creativity, however, that allows us to rise above desperate days, bouts with illness, and lost love. It gives us our most essential tool for well-being. By using the power of our imaginations and creativity, we can overcome our limitations and our negative responses to life.

Have you thought about doing something creative, but felt you were not creative enough? Have you felt so tied up with things that the time for your creative expression has always been pushed to the next month, the next year, or the next century! Then the *fire time* is now. Get the matches, and let's move to a new place, where life has all the fire you need. I once asked a group that I was leading in a seminar on creativity: how far did they have to travel to feel that they had traveled? Although there can be many answers to this question, it could be *not very far at all*, since your mind has the potential of immediately taking you to any place you want. Edgar Rice Burroughs never traveled to Africa, yet his tales of adventure with Tarzan are extraordinary and filled with excitement, mystery, and joy. This fiercely charismatic man, with one commanding yell, could make animals come to greet him. Each of us has the yell we need inside of us. Each of us can explore the forests and jungles of our minds. In the following pages, I will offer you ways to navigate your forest or jungle. It is easier with a guide, someone who can point out the signs you need to see and the sounds you need to pay attention to. It is so easy to lose your way and get lost. Often the creative impulse needs a guide; otherwise it might wither and die.

Some believe that creativity is an innate skill or quality that cannot be learned or expanded. After fifteen years of teaching people how to be more creative, I am confident that this is not the case. I believe that anyone who gets through the daily emergencies and stresses of life is already showing great creativity. Often we are more creative than we realize. However, we so often downplay our unique ability to get through things.

As long as you can light a match, you can learn to express yourself more creatively. It's easy. And once you light that match, you will never want to go back to the darkness. You will never want to leave the warmth of the fire. You will find that your creative expression—whether it is in writing, drawing, sculpting, photographing, painting, etc.—will give you a meaning of life which you may have lost when you came of age.

When I was sixteen, I remember staring out of my friend's apartment window after a summer rain and smelling the wonderful fresh smell of wet-dry dirt. The trees were so very green with their coating of rainwater. The air had a cleanness that I have never forgotten. These special and lasting moments felt so safe and comforting, as if the world were opening up to me. They have never left me. How has that memory shaped my life? What new meaning lies within, which might unfold as I explore with writing or image-making? What thoughts might rise out of the quietness of a blank page? What adolescent or adult memories might slip into consciousness? It is as easy as lighting a match. Your memories set the mood for a stroll through your mind to seek your story, so you can awaken the creative flow of your being. Exploring your creativity becomes a gift that gives you more than you could ever have imagined at the striking.

All new steps in new directions require decisions. Until you decide to explore, you will always wonder what it would have been like if you had made the decision to approach your creative self. The value of the decision is health. The value of the decision is reaching up onto the cave wall of your mind and drawing the fearsome animals, as our ancestors did—so you can capture and explore the meaning of the life experience and allay the fears, angers, and frustrations that sometimes cause *dis-ease* in our bodies. There is satisfaction in writing down your thoughts, in drawing the images that you see, and in creating something that is all yours, from your own hands. Creativity expands with exercise. Creativity expands with the decision to do creative acts. And, as you believe in your creativity, you expand it. Instead of just watching the sunrise, you might decide to paint it. Instead of just passing an interesting face, you might photograph it. It is easy to begin. Once you decide, the process becomes easier. Time will always continue to slip away. Contain it with your writing, your drawings, and your photographs. Record the moments, and you will discover the satisfying world of self-expression and the story that is uniquely yours. Decide to be creative, and awaken the world within. It is for your benefit.

We so often put aside things that might help us to be fulfilled and whole—which would allow us to have an outlet for our frustrations and anger so that we could remain healthy and confident. Over the years, I have thought that if people were to explore their creative natures more, they might be healthier and look forward to more days. As we go through our daily routines, we seem to get used to seeing dreary faces, disguised faces, or I-know-you-are-looking faces. But do we see faces that are truly present and vital, because there is something about the environment or life that sparks their interest or their curiosity? And how do we confront our difficult days? Is it with cool sarcasm or an angry word or two? When was the last time you used Crayola to boldly draw a funny figure to soothe your disquieting day or scribbled all over a white page with gusto, using red and, perhaps, yellow crayon, or made your face up as at Halloween to play a ghoulish character? It might seem strange, but these silly spontaneous activities help to loosen your encrusted creativity.

I remember being so intrigued with some of the faces that I had seen actors create with makeup that I asked an actor friend of mine to make my face up for the stage. In jest, I hope, he made me up into a profoundly evil-looking villain. I was so struck by my appearance that I had dinner with my friend at a local restaurant with the disguise still on. I found it so fascinating to be this character that I stayed in makeup for two days!

We may not be as far from our primitive ancestors as we think. But we definitely enjoy exploring the parts of ourselves that are hard to define and which are filled with creative play. As tough as it sometimes is growing up, there are always games to play and fun to be had. Any object can be transformed by our imagination and our need to have it fit whatever we are playing. A stick can be a sword, a machine gun, or a spear. From ancient days there have always been toys constructed by imaginative play. All kinds of dolls have been dug up at archaeological sites in different parts of the world. Some have been made of wood; others have been of straw. Some even had human hair. Cherish your childish heart, and bring out the games that inspired you when you were young. It is so wonderful to let the fun out of your box of crayons. I remember getting my first box of sixty-four. There was joy in all those colors! The task was to use each color in one picture, so it looked good. Crayola awakens your imagination and helps you complete your wheel of wholeness.

Completing the wheel and completing yourself can be easy. It's lighting the match. It's making the decision to explore. You complete the wheel when you exercise your creativity and explore your wonderful imaginative inner world. The power we hold within us is awe inspiring, but many of us go through our lives without tapping into it. This depository is filled with stories, images, jewels of thought, and the magic of your life that is waiting for you when you address your wheel. It's your circle of life, your journey that wraps around and comes back to the beginning of things. It is interesting that the further we get from our youth the more we view it and its many facets. It is as if we are answering the question posed by the band Talking Heads: "How did I get here?" "Letting the days go by …" is what David Byrne sings, as if it is a mindless repetition of days. And it could be that way, but now is the time to mindfully and creatively approach the passing of time and make it truly meaningful and beautiful. We have the ability to do it, to complete the wheel.

When I was in my teens, I loved reading about artists, whether they were painters, writers, or sculptors. Gauguin, van Gogh, Picasso, Hemingway, Jean-Paul Sartre, Rodin, and Moore were names that spun all kinds of magic and wonder in my mind. I wanted that wonderful creative life for myself. But how? I did not know, because there was no real "go for broke" drive in me to become an artist. I needed to work to make a living. Having grown up in the streets of New York, the most important activity for me was a job. Money was more important than creative expression. As time passed, I drifted further and further away from that dream of being an artist. I thought it was reality that took over. I felt I was being responsible, and art was for the artist, anyway. But as I grew older, I realized that the need to create was not only still there, but it was struggling to come out. As I began teaching and working with many people, I came to realize that I was not alone. There are many people who have this same urge to express themselves creatively who are just waiting to find a way to do it. From what I have experienced, I think the need to create is within us all. The question is: how often do we express it? Frequently we are stopped by fear—the fear of not being good enough, of not having the talent, or of just drifting into the future without dealing with this important part of ourselves. It might be all of these things, but time can lead us into a corner, where we must finally express what has traveled through our veins too long unspoken.

Creativity breathes life into the weakest soul. It fosters a renewal of energy and vision. If it is utilized, it will make you healthier; if it is not utilized, it could drag you into the maelstrom of disease. My suggestion is always to grab the pen, the brush, the colors, the music sheets—and begin! In the quiet of a Sunday morning, begin exploring your history, your story. Do you want to write about it? Begin. Is there a scene from your past that comes to your mind periodically? Draw it, even if you do not know how. Review your experiences, and start a journal, or make a verbal recording of your memories that you can later give to your children. There are so many ways to express your individual vision.

I remember that as a kid I wanted to be a cowboy. I had the six-guns and the holster and the dream of traveling to the West on a beautiful white horse. I would lead a wagon train and enjoy the open range, along with the nightly howl of the coyote. We would share food and tell tales over a campfire, smelling the richness of the earth and the burnt odor of the wood and the smoke. It may be one of the reasons why I like camping as much as I do. I also wanted to heroically save a damsel in distress. Where are my six-guns!

But, more importantly, where are yours? What childhood dreams still linger? What secret yearning still resides within your chest? These are such assets to your creative life and expression. Use them to help you to start thinking and imagining. Let them be your jump-off point into a more creative experience. Drawing takes but a single line and then another and another—a curve here and a straight line there. Before you realize where you are going, you have a drawing. It is the same with writing. One word and then another and another, and, before you know it, you have a series of sentences leading you through the engaging forest of your mind. There is such value to you that it would have been a shame if you had remained silent—even for yourself.

The stoking of creativity can occur with the simplest of actions. It requires only that you initially choose something and then do it on a regular basis. It could be every Sunday afternoon, for instance. It would become your time to complete the wheel, to sequester yourself from the "madding crowd" and expose petal by petal the creative energy that has been pent up in you for so long. A wheel is such a wonderful image, symbolic of the beginning and the end all wrapped together—of seasons, of unity, of progress, of Mother Earth and the magic of the creative mind. When you join in the creative thrust of things, you become one in harmony with the universe, evolving and enriching in the flow of energy that is a part of everything. When we hold ourselves back, or allow the mundane things of life to control us and not allow us our moments of individual expression, we become dulled to the details of life. We "see" without seeing; we are on automatic, our minds follow by rote, and we see only what we want to see, leaving so much unobserved. I had a student who came out of her apartment every day and passed a lovely group of flowers. She never noticed them until she was given a photographic assignment directing her to explore her immediate environment. She could not believe that she had missed them. What nuances have you missed lately? What extraordinarily obvious things have you missed? It is so easy to miss things when we become half-conscious through daily routines that, by their boredom, rob us of being truly aware. Repetition can be helpful as well as mind-numbing. Certainly it is useful, but it also can prevent us from being in the moment. Enjoyment often comes from savoring what is right before you, whether it is a flower, a child, or the beauty of light brazenly coming through a wide green and white leaf. Beauty speaks in a moment of "seeing and realizing." Your time—our time—passes so quickly, but with a creative wand we can slow it down and make note of its many wonders. To be conscious and to be aware of being conscious are extraordinary gifts that your art and your creativity can give you. When you capture the leaf, with all its texture and color and wonder, it is an extraordinary moment.

We struggle in life to keep things in balance. So often, however, things enter that throw our balance off, and we become anxious and disturbed by this intrusion. We wonder how we are going to get things back to a state of equilibrium. It is one of the wonders of art that it offers a way to use this disorder of feelings and wayward thoughts and to construct and creatively channel it into an expression that brings us back to internal balance. Our creative expression provides us with a meaningful way to deal with the problems of life that many times can cause us great pain and illness. The importance of this process cannot be overemphasized. I remember a woman, Julie, who was attending one of my seminars, and she was going through a very difficult period with her health. She had been diagnosed with breast cancer. The shock of it nearly crushed her spirit, but, with the help of her husband and the fact that she became totally involved with expressing herself through the photography projects that we were doing, she stayed present and vital and did not give in to the despair that she had felt at the beginning of her struggle with the disease. Attempting things creative has a way of absorbing you and pulling you into the wonder of the act or process. Julie eventually went into remission. She was very grateful for the opportunity the workshops gave her to do something that not only kept her mind off the treatments but gave her a greater appreciation of the world around her. She saw things more completely through the lens of her camera. It is easy to miss the wonder and beauty around us when we become so caught up in a fast-moving world. Our creative expression slows the world down, so that we can actually see it more clearly, with more intensity and more awareness of its texture and sound.

I love the concept of the wheel. How well do we roll through life? How do we go over the bumps in the road? How much effort have we put into keeping our wheels turning? There are some people who have not oiled their wheels in years. They are squeaking and moaning through their days. And, in some cases, they are disappointed in life and do not know what to do to quiet the boredom and monotony that seems to confront them regularly. They have a feeling that they are missing something, but they can't quite decide what it is. Although a quiet beach with spirited waves and resolute birds can give you a sense of peace and renewal, a quick drawing of the scene, or a photograph, or a word picture could give you this setting at other moments to help you through more difficult days. If you are inspired by the scene, capture it, so that you have it for the future, so that you do not forget the beauty and specialness of that moment of your life. I have a drawing I did of a garden outside a living room that I always loved to sit in. The lighting, and the outside furniture, and the trees, and flowers, and bushes were so restful and delightful. I am sure I must have thought that I would just remember this little piece of earth. But memory is unreliable. It comes in spurts and sometimes not at all. I am so glad I did not leave that scene to my memory, that I was able to slowly and awkwardly, through the use of a pencil and white paper, transcribe the garden I saw through the sliding glass door. It was not about my skill at drawing that made me do it. It was my desire to creatively capture what I saw and loved, while I also oiled the wheel. I later framed this spontaneous creative adventure, so that I could go back to the peaceful mornings that I had spent drinking coffee and gazing out at that delightful garden.

Completing the wheel is about exploring your moments, both during the actual experience, as well as artistically, later, to bring it all back to be reviewed and savored. Life goes by quickly. We need to reflect and visit times in our lives, so we have a strong sense of meaning and purpose to its unfolding. We all see things differently. Some see without really "seeing." Others see, but with limited vision. We all need to practice expanding our vision, so that we can appreciate more, so that we see more details—more of whom we are and what we think. Sometimes we think that we cannot write creatively because we have nothing to say. It is not until the pen hits that paper that our hidden thoughts suddenly emerge and surprise us with their unfolding tale. We regularly underestimate ourselves. It is one of the reasons we have broken spokes in our wheels. We may be earning a living, exercising, eating well, taking care of our spiritual side, and having a good family life—but not taking the time to unlock the part of us that seeks creative expression. It is this part that sometimes speaks to you at night, which causes unrest and a feeling that you need something more—some way of discovering what the hell is bothering you when nothing really should. In the quietness, you wonder what you could do that might make you feel more fulfilled. In the years I have been teaching people, I have seen over and over again that involvement with some kind of creative expression changes people's experience with their lives, and they become enchanted with their developing creativity. Even a crayoned drawing can lift you from where you are in your life to a whole new place of goals and expectations. I have asked people to close their eyes and think about an imaginary place that would make them feel immediately happy and somehow fulfilled. Diane, one of my students, drew a farm with a house, and horses, and flowers, and sunshine. And she said this was exactly what she had been wanting for such a long time. "It is only seeing it now in my drawing that I realize how much I want to leave city life and move to the county." Within two years, she realized her dream!

The creativity that is within each of us is always ready to appear if we will let it—if we will give it the opportunity to come out from hiding, so that it can renew our spirits and our lives. It is all up to us. I find that people will often deny this essential part, because it seems too childish and ungrown-up. To suddenly draw with crayons, or write with pencil in a journal, speaks too much of the joys of childhood with its spontaneous games and imaginary friends. It is interesting how so much of our joy as children came from these wonderful explorations of imagination and childish games and that we hesitate to utilize these "tools for living" as we get older. Has maturity robbed us of our natural expressions of life? Having watched so many people over the years reunite with their creative selves, I know the joy and the satisfaction that comes with this rejoining of parts. We too readily relinquish our rights to play, to give ourselves over to the freedom of being childlike again. It is in our best interest to overcome this neglect of ourselves. Children do not concern themselves with the importance or the meaning of the task or game. It is just the playing of it that makes the difference. "Do you want to play pirates?" Of course you do.

Striking the Match

Buy a box of crayons and some construction paper, so that they are your own. Then, use them to begin your journey. First, draw a place where you would most like to be or visit. Then write on the back of the drawing what that image means to you. The others drawings are up to you.

CREATIVE SPOKE
Chapter Two

Lightning and thunder can set your mind in a whirl. As a small child, I was afraid of summer storms. My mother would come to comfort me, so I could be soothed and tenderly rescued from this ancient fear. In time, however, I have come to enjoy the sudden bursts of light and the loud booming of thunder. Sometimes the beauty and power of the storm hold me transfixed, caught in its amazing natural expression. As the clouds have gathered, so must you also gather your experiences and pictures and memories and construct the spokes that are needed to complete your wheel of health and natural expression. Plato suggested that the unexamined life is not worth living. So gather it all up: your storms, your lightning, your collection of pieces and bits of things, and use them in your new, rich exploration of your creative self. Dip into the kaleidoscopic mixture, so that you can bring forth your own telling of the story.

I remember as a child using the hills and crannies of the bedding to play cowboys and Indians—plastic figures waiting behind imaginary rocks to suddenly attack the wagon train, or the cavalry chasing renegades, or, perhaps, a shootout between two opposing figures. The fastest draw would win—of course, that was me! It was fun to play for hours enjoying the miniature display of the mythological West. As we get older, we move away from these delightful moments of play to become serious adults. However, I believe we have pulled away from the most important part of ourselves—our joy for play and our enthusiasm for our imaginary world. So come with me now to those wonderful yesterdays filled with adventure, and reach out to the child within, so that you can again enjoy the richness of imagination and creativity—not necessarily to honor the past, but to vitalize the present and profoundly affect the future.

Consider for a moment the spokes of your wheel. What does each of the spokes represent? What is it that keeps you rolling through life? What is it that you strive to have in this life? Certainly health, happiness, love, friendships, family, and success all fall within the scope of your dreams, if not your reality. What we do to achieve them varies with our understanding and our ability to engage in creative variations. When we were children, none of the plastic figures were just dead. They each were able to rise again, to carry on the good fight. A toy figure might transform into a scout, rustler, farmer, lone rider, Indian chief, or Marshall and develop a whole new story, a whole new plan. We can learn from this childhood creativity. It gives us a way to understand how we can pull from the ashes a whole new way of interpreting our health, love, family, etc. The strength of a relationship is dependent upon the openness of the communication. But more important than that is the variance of the communication. The question is: Do we have the flexibility to still come up with the transformations and variations of communications, to assign new labels to things to change the story, to revitalize the engagement and realign our thinking so that we can be more effective? Many of us, with the passing years, lose the God-given beauty of our imaginative childhood mind. We become confined to the box of established routines, habits, practicalities, and I-know-better frames of reference. The wheel goes out of kilter, and the life road becomes rocky and less responsive to our desires and goals. We minimize our childish games only at our own expense. They are our lifeblood for overcoming obstacles, breakups, failures, and mishaps.

The wheel presents an interesting concept for evaluating our lives and their balances. The wheel is ancient. Its ability to carry us through our mental journeys is woven into our universal connections, so that we can grasp the importance of keeping our balance. There is no doubt that we slip, that we drift from our tasks of keeping the spokes in repair and the wheel balanced—which then affects our lives and their many manifestations. If we were to put our health in one of the spokes of our wheel, would we be able to show that we have taken care of it? Have we given it enough exercise and nourishing food to maintain this important spoke? Or is the spoke worn and ill fitting, and about to cause us some discomfort, throwing us off balance? What is true of the health spoke is also true of the creativity spoke. If it is not tended to, it becomes unreliable, causing us to lose interest in many things around us. We begin to feel out of balance and uncomfortable inside. We sometimes seek something that will bring us into alignment with ourselves and quiet the dissatisfaction that springs from deep within us. I believe our dissatisfaction comes from our loss of the creative energy that is generated from within. Without this primary force, we struggle with ourselves, trying to discover how to overcome our ennui, our failing relationships, or our unsatisfying jobs. During these times of distress and uncertainty, we get locked up within ourselves and lose the flexibility to see clearly and do something constructive about it. I believe it is so important to have our creative selves open and energized to help us through these strains on your life.

Opening our creative selves allows us to see more clearly and to come up with more possible answers and responses. If nothing else, it gives us a way to express our dissatisfaction with the present situations. Overcoming difficulties is a state of mind that is fostered by creativity. One of the practices that can get our creativity moving again is journal writing. Although it is a practice that seems to be more and more suggested, it is seldom followed with any regularity; only a few people take the time to uncover its value and magic. I had a woman in my Journal Writing class a few years back who was concerned with aging and the loss of things that had previously made her feel good. She was a reluctant participant in the workshop and came as a result of having nothing else to do on this one particular Saturday. She had decided she would sit in for just a bit and see what would be said that might stir her interest. I explained the richness of writing down your thoughts. I told of the wonderful things that we miss about ourselves when we have not written our thoughts down to revisit at a later date. I spoke about how quickly we can lose a really good idea or thought if we have not written it down so that we can review it later. She began doing the assignments and coming regularly. It was wonderful to see her move from being a hesitant member of the biweekly group to a motivated journal writer willing to expose her thoughts and feelings. In writing about her hesitations and fears, she released in others their own concerns and discomforts, so that all could freely participate in this group with openness and truth. It lifted the other members out of their own limitations and thoughts of inadequacy. So often remarks such as: "I just can't write," "I have nothing to say," and "It's all been said before" rob us of the opportunity to expose our creativity and the thoughts that can be so helpful to us. We fail many times to realize that whatever we say has never been said in precisely *our* way. It has never been expressed through *our* eyes and from *our* experiences. We all have gifts we have not utilized. Writing is something that we all can do. Writing just needs to be approached and practiced. As our wonderful group wrote more and more, the joy of living reached out from each of the pages that we read. We traveled deeply into the recesses of our experiences to explore our creative souls. Each of us felt reflected in the others. The fear of aging was no longer hidden in the corners of an isolated individual but now was a part of a community that felt the emotion and the struggle to overcome its grip with a renewed strength and forbearance—we found the gift of sharing.

I remember sitting in a barbershop shortly after my mother died and suddenly feeling overcome with grief and anxiety. I could not place where the anxiety was coming from or the fit of nervous twitching that spontaneously took over my hands. I was in a cold sweat. All I could think about was how I would explain to the barber what was taking place. I finally blamed it on my job. I had been working at a bar in Queens, on Northern Boulevard, at the time and decided that it was this highly active and rowdy place that had caused this disruption between my hands and mind. But, in truth, it was my unspoken realization that my mother was totally gone from my life. And it wasn't until years later, while I was doing a seminar, that this experience came back to me, and I was able to release it through writing down all the pent-up emotions that had lain hidden within the recesses of my mind throughout the passing years.

There is so much within us. We are adventures within adventures. There are so many layers to our minds and memories, which we can only reach through some kind of creative expression that will bring us through its labyrinth to an awakening of self. We sometimes reach a point in our lives when we wonder what else we can tap into to reinvent ourselves, to develop a more interesting and inviting job or pastime activity, and to keep us pulsating and finding the wonder in this life. It is when we get caught in those moments of struggle and dissatisfaction that investigating our creative selves becomes so important.

The value of a journal cannot be overemphasized. It offers you a recording of history—*your* history. It delves into the wonder and complexity of your thoughts and feelings. What better way to confront yourself, to find what you really believe, your philosophy of living? There are times when life reaches out and gives you a nasty jolt. You find yourself spinning and not knowing what to do to keep yourself together. Your journal gives you that place to review, to rethink, and to reinvestigate the situation. It gives you an opportunity to revisit a past experience—as long as you have taken the time to write it down.

I had a woman called Sarah few years ago in one of my seminars, who had been going through a very difficult time with her boyfriend. She was at a point of not knowing what to do. I suggested to her that she start a journal and let the floodgates open. She took my advice and did start. She wrote down all her thoughts about the relationship in her new journal. It spilled out in a dynamic rush of emotions and thoughts. It gave her a place to vent, to curse, to rage, and to cry. The release was dramatic and heart wrenching, but it allowed for so much of the pain and personal retribution to flow *out* instead of being locked *in* to fester and control and then develop into some future *dis-order*. She was so happy that she had done this process. Did it change the situation? No. What it did change was her point of view and all the emotions that were bound to the experience of the relationship. It gave her a way of seeing it more clearly. It gave her a way to recognize how it was not providing her with what she wanted. And it gave her a way of moving on. We all need that reflection on our life experiences. Get the journal and begin. It can be so very helpful in your journey.

When we were three years old, it was so easy to draw, to take the crayons and color the page with lines that would squiggle and spin and almost look like something. The great joy of showing those spontaneous expressions was the delight of the day as your parent or grandparent "wowed" and smiled and kissed your head. Orange, yellow, and green mixed in a rectangular sky spoke of the imagination's ability to transcend reality, to construct a world where anything was possible—even a random assortment of lines contributed to an individual's development. But, now that we are older, we shy away from our early beginnings and deny ourselves this exploration of line and color and imagination as if it were beyond us. I have heard so often, "Oh, I can't draw."

"Ever?" is always my response. What happened to the childhood years when hours drifted away in the wonder of construction paper, crayons, and shapes? What beauty did we discover there? What colorful expression did we tap into that went beyond the immediate moment to give us a glimpse of ourselves and showed us a relationship between ourselves and the rest of the world? The sun, with yellow lines randomly coming out of a yellow circle, brightly staring down at the sprawling brown and green land that we had peopled with oversized heads and awkward bodies was our attempt to order and place things in our environment and in our minds. To ignore this creative spoke of your wheel is to prevent it from exposing its secrets and its beauty, and, perhaps, even its ugliness. When you draw, it is not necessary that you draw like an artist. But it is necessary to see what happens inside you, as you introduce this experience back into your life. You might be surprised how engaging this expression can be for you. I have had moments when time slipped peacefully by as I drew something that had captured my attention. It might have been a plant, a window, a garden, or a beach with the ocean rolling in with bubbles of white foam. These moments are like a meditation that allows you to rest in the creation of an image.

I remember watching television a few years ago and being really absorbed by an interview with Edward Albee, the playwright. While watching, I picked up a pencil and one of my children's old drawing pads and started doodling. Before I realized what I was doing, I was just totally engaged in trying to capture his face, not for any purpose other than that it was so absorbing to do it. When the program ended, I was surprised that I had spent the entire hour just sketching this man's face. I have since encouraged many students to lift a pencil, grab a drawing pad, and discover for themselves something in their environment that strikes them, captures their interest, and creates a response within them. This spontaneous expression gives rise to a link that can lead to the recesses of your mind. An unfolding can take place to bring alive the precious gift that we all possess but seldom utilize—our creativity.

One student I had was very adamant that she could not draw and that she had no artistic abilities. I recommended a book and also suggested how relaxing it could be to just sit and draw for a while. After a number of encouragements, she finally began to draw from photographic images. She was hesitant and slightly aggravated but continued with one drawing after another, until she began to become absorbed by the doing of it. There was a quiet challenge that reached into another part of her mind, which became excited by this new endeavor. She has since moved to using pastels and paints and creating the most wonderful works of art. This was someone who was convinced that she did not have any creativity within her. And yet, once she began, she not only found she could draw but that she could draw beyond what she could have ever conceived before she took the chance. It is so important to explore yourself creatively.

Not long ago, I did a presentation to a group of seniors. When I suggested that we were going to use crayons to draw, I was viewed as if I had just lost my grip on reality. Through their nodding heads and vocal nays, they asserted that they did not draw nor would they do it with crayons. Thankfully, they humored me and completed the exercise that I had asked them to do. To their wonderful surprise, not only did they enjoy their drawings, but they discovered insights about themselves from what they had written about the drawings. They had never imagined that such a simple assignment would produce so many interesting insights into themselves. We have within us a wealth of information and images that will come out as long as we give it the opportunity to come out. So don't hold back! Get the crayons. Get the pencil. Get the drawing pad, and explore.

So often we hold back and do not release the power that is part of our nature and our souls. Drawing is an opportunity to join with the past in a way that will revitalize the present. The child in you wants to reach out and give you a hand, so that you can enjoy the simple things again and find joy in your natural expression.

Of course, there are times when you will want to hesitate. I remember when I was about six years old (and living in the Bronx, and believing that anything was possible), that I considered showing some of my disbelieving friends that I could, indeed, fly. In particular I wanted to show Ralph, who was always the first to say that it could not be done. I remember going to my parents' third-floor apartment, walking through the length of it to the bedroom window, and picking up a small blanket before going out the window onto the iron fire escape to show my skill at flying. If Superman could do it, there was no reason why I should not be able to do it as well, I thought. As I stood on the edge of the fire escape and looked down at my friends gathered below, I wondered if I had overstepped myself. After all, I had not actually done this before. At this point, one of my friends said, "Are you really going to jump?" I said yes with firmness and decisiveness. I am asking *you* to say yes with firmness and decisiveness as well—even if you are not sure of the outcome. It is worth the risk. It is worth seeing what drawings you will develop as you use the implements you have chosen to express the reflections of your mind's eye. A wonderful book to help you in this journey is Frederick Franck's *The Zen of Seeing*. It is one of those books that should not be missed.

Another practice to provoke your creativity is photography, which can give you instant gratification in your quest for a new expressive form. Photography opens you up to the details of the world. It gives you an opportunity to explore and see and do things with the joy of a final copy. To visually capture an image is to confine a moment of your experience, so that it can be reviewed in the future, so that it can be revisited in the quietness of thought. This is a wonderful characteristic of this boxed magic. You can review the details of a flower or an expression of a lover so that you can relive the memory, so that you can glean some new information or beauty from that time captured. Sometimes things go by too quickly. Sometimes they go by so fast we miss them. But with a camera you can prevent the total loss of the party, of your daughter's expression at Christmas, of your son's graduation, or the seminar you attended. It all can be recorded for your enrichment. Our memories are imperfect transcribers. But with photography you can bring back the details and enjoy the past.

Photography has more intrigue to it than we might at first perceive. What it presents is not as obvious as it seems. It is revealing, not only in the images that you have captured, but in its revelations about you. It gives you clues about who you are and what you see and how you feel. I remember when I first started taking photographs. The camera seemed so difficult, so demanding. I was always afraid I would mess things up, so I became very hesitant about touching the dials. They seemed so mysterious and profound. Today, however, with digital photography, everything is so much easier, and the photographs come out great on automatic. The old drawbacks to taking pictures are gone. You can now use your camera as a tool to explore without worrying about the dials. Just snap. The question is, on this journey of yours, what do you snap? You need to snap anything that is truly meaningful to you, anything that emotionally moves you. For it is from the things that attract your attention, that *engage* you, that you will learn the most.

A student of mine photographed a sled that was leaning against the front of a home. There was a white fence in front of the sled, which was included in the image. He didn't think much of it until I reviewed it in class. I thought it was interesting that he had left the fence in instead of choosing a different angle so that he could see the sled more directly, as another student had. This interference, you could say, was just an accident. There was no thought involved in leaving the fence in. As he said, it just happened. But as he thought about the image, he realized that there was a lot more to it than he had originally thought. He realized that the fence actually prevented him from seeing the whole sled clearly. So why had he not seen the fence, or why had he ignored the fence? As he thought about it, he realized that he allowed things to block him, that he overlooked things that he should pay attention to. What is true in life is that we see—what we want to see—and we eliminate what we do not want to see. It is interesting how often people say, after they look at a picture that they have taken, "I didn't see that when I was taking the picture." What have you missed? What have you missed and not recognized as missing?

Photography is an intriguing tool to bring you closer to yourself and what you see and think. It also enlarges your scope if you explore your internal responses to the images when you are viewing them. Although it is not usually thought of this way, photography can be a journey into the symbols of your life. A whole new language can come from your collection of photographs. What have you selected to photograph? Why was that moment, scene, or person so important to you? What thoughts come back to you as you focus on the image? It is interesting to see how a single image can bring back so many memories. The whole experience is suddenly before you again with all its joy, regrets, and longing. These moments of reflection can reorient you and bring you to a greater truth about who you are and where you are going.

I recently found again a photo I had taken years ago of the bottom staircase of the apartment building I grew up in. It showed the stairs that led up to the third floor, which was the longest flight. When I first looked at the photo, I could not figure out why I had taken this photograph. And then it came to me in a rush. When I was six years old, I used to jump from the top step straight down to the hallway floor below. It was a long way! I remember wondering, when I took this image: *What was I thinking that possessed me to dare the length of it?* And I realized that there was something inside of me that made me dare myself to do things that I was initially afraid of. The image symbolically represents something that took me so many years to recognize about myself and my behavior.

Exploring your old photographs and producing new ones can unlock your imagination and your creativity. It can offer you a way to go beyond your usual thinking as well as offer you a way to see more clearly. What limits you is continuing to think in the same way. Your creative part, once exposed, will open you up to all the wonder that is you.

I'm going to fly

Striking the Match

Pull out your old photographs and see them with new eyes of discovery, as if they are a foreign land to be enjoyed and researched. Reflect on the images, and see what secrets lie hidden within their borders.

Pick up your camera or cell phone and capture the moments; capture images that attract your attention. Give reign to your creative side, and play the artistic photographer. Have fun with this new role of explorer.

In addition, grab your pencil or pen and transcribe your thoughts within the covers of a journal. Let your mind wander over the plains of your mind and imagination, and see what comes up. You could even throw in a drawing or two. There is only one good time to begin. That time is now!

FIRE AND IRON
Chapter Three

Fire has a mesmerizing affect on us. To gaze into the fire is to drift off into some hidden world, where reverie overcomes the moment and we see pictures of past experiences dancing as ancient people used to dance. When a sound or a voice suddenly intrudes, we realize we have not been present for a while. To hide our startledness, we smile and try to respond with some meaningful expression. However, we have been caught, and there is certain sadness to the movement of time. In that mesmerizing glimpse we became aware of the forces that moved us—except that we saw this as a transgression and not as a window into our history, our stories, our creativity, and our souls. It is fire that binds metals together. It is the fire of reverie that binds our memories together and ignites our creative expression, so that we can overcome the iron nature of logic and our locked rigidity of thought. What is it that releases our creativity? Capturing our wandering minds does, to the extent that we learn from it and allow reverie to stay fired for a while. The only way to escape the rigidity of our expected thoughts is to sharpen our awareness of our transgressing ones and savor those to build on in a new direction.

I remember once waiting in a huge living room for someone, before we went out, and unexpectedly being interested in some bamboo plants growing from a vase of water. They reached out in circular movements toward a high ceiling. I suddenly thought that I would like to draw them. It was a ridiculous thought. But I got a piece of paper and a pencil and did it to the best of my limited ability. I still have the drawing. It represents a move in a new direction. It symbolizes the power of a thought that I would have normally discarded, but which in this instance gave me a vision of something else that I could do. It was another way of expressing a moment without losing it, perhaps forever. This was my second drawing since childhood. I became aware of how much the comfort of the room and that person had come to mean to me in that isolated expression. I look back, at times, and I am grateful that I took the chance to do what I would normally have rejected. In the reverie of the drawing, I found a meaning that I could easily have missed. You do not want to miss these moments of spontaneous innovation and expansion.

Sometimes a dream fragment can catch our attention and send us to an unknown area of our brain to momentarily drift and wander. It is important to use those moments and record them in some way, so that they can help us to more firmly encourage our creativeness. In dreams, we are already dealing with a symbolism that reaches into the very core of human imagination. Do not neglect this rich source of material. Even if you feel that you never dream, start the practice of preparing for a dream thread. It may not be available right away, but, with expectation, it will suddenly appear one morning, to your delighted surprise. Dreams will awaken your intrigue with puzzles and who-done-its. For example, how is it that the girlfriend of his wife was able to kill Mary, his wife, during a time when he was out shopping? The question is: Did he know Mary's girlfriend before the murder? I immediately thought that he had known her. But then again, maybe he did not. Of course, we are not sure. And so it goes....

A dream fragment, with its twists and turns, can leave us guessing for a long time. Dreams can be such an interesting entry for your journal. I remember waking up not long ago retaining a fragment of a dream. I was following someone, and she suddenly disappeared ahead of me. I tried to catch up, but she was nowhere to be seen. As I came over the crest of a very high hill, I could not see her, or anyone, and the incline was very steep. You know how dreams are. I suddenly slipped and started sliding toward an opening which would plunge me down hundreds of feet. I just barely caught a foothold along a jutting rock. I was not able to grab on to anything else so I could pull myself away from the deadly opening. I realized that I was very close to falling and woke up with a jolt. Thank God, since I had been just about to go over the edge into empty space. In the days that followed, I thought about who the woman might be. Why did she leave me? How could she leave me in such a precarious position? Why did I seem weak as my life hung in the balance? What would have happened if I had fallen? Did this have any meaning to my real life? What matters is not necessarily the answers to the questions but just the play of it all. Playing with different meanings, so that you can come to a greater understanding of the forces within you, as well as exploring your creative nature, is essential to the process. This can be one of the most effective ways of developing your imagination and expanding your creativity. We all get stuck, at one point or another, with how to engage and develop our creativeness. With practice, this investigation into your dreams can lead you to new discoveries as well as expand a part of yourself that often lies dormant. Reflect on your dreams, and bridge an important gap between imagination and reality.

Rain is such a wonderful inducer for reverie, for wandering without bounds. A good storm has all the elements essential for drifting in thought: the splashing of rain hitting into things, including its own puddles, so there is this slapping noise along with intermittent thunder. Loud, sudden thunder always brings me back to childhood. There are times I can smell the wet grass and dirt just as I did when I was a kid: the clean smell of air drenched in sweet rainwater. Pelham Bay Park, in the Bronx, was a place my father would take me so that we could do something together; we'd play catch, or tag, or just walk. I hated just walking. But with two six-guns strapped to my waist, I could at least shoot the bad guys. My father always smiled as I suddenly sprang to action and shot the bad guys that had been hiding behind trees along our walk. I saved my dad any number of times.

One Saturday morning after the rain, my dad gave me a box kite as a surprise. We weren't sure if it was going to fly, since everything was so wet. However, there was a concrete stadium with steps and seats that I used to love running up and down. We decided we should go to the top of the stadium and run with it up there, since it was already higher in the sky and not as wet. Well, my dad tried for about ten minutes or so, running back and forth, hoping to get it to lift and catch some wind. There was hardly a breeze, so my dad gave up. I asked if I could do it. He smiled and said that I could try but if he could not get it to fly, I might not be able to as well. I also ran back and forth at the top of this concrete stadium for an unbelievably long time. My dad had suggested many times to stop and let it be; we could come back when there was more wind. Just one more time, I would say over and over again. Just one more. Finally, after the fifteenth "just one more," the kite took off, and the string slipped easily off the roller. It went higher and higher. What a great sight! I was crazed with joy. My dad congratulated me. Persistence had won the day. The box kite flew—and I was wedded to a memory that only reappeared when I started the practice of exploring images and memories that arose by a clap of thunder or the cool spill of rain on my arms.

My father died when I was twelve. Many memories were buried with him—until I could let my mind wander like the box kite and could be lifted from my forgetfulness. It brought to light the beauty of our relationship, even in its briefness.

Give yourself over to the rain and its penchant for reverie. It will foster your connections to the beauty of your past. Use persistence to overcome the darkness that clouds your memories, so that the richness of your life can be unfolded to make your story known.

Fire and water transform each other. Our memories and dreams transform us as well. They can act to inspire, to calm, to enflame, or to soothe us. We feel ourselves drawn to these elements, because they enliven us. They bring us back to our essential nature. We come from a swarming mass of nutrients and water. We reach out of our ancient beginnings to engage in the rituals of fire, so that we can produce energy and creativity. As soon as we no longer engage in these forces, we begin to decline in spirit and in energy. We begin to lounge too long. Sometimes we accept too easily the changes of life and give in to the loneliness of repetitive days. We become iron-like, inflexible, and lacking in regenerative spirit. The importance of our creativity cannot be overemphasized. We begin to leave ourselves when we lose the creative spirit—which is why it is so important to stir the ashes of memory and pool the liquidity of reverie, so that we can maintain our energy and our desire to look forward to our intriguing future, where it all comes together. When we see how difficult people's lives are sometimes, it is obvious that concentration on the present can be debilitating. I learned a long time ago, during a ropes course, to focus on where I was going rather than looking down from where I was—which was forty feet off the ground! Creating a different future comes out of using the natural forces that are part of our nature to continue reaching and bending with the storms. When we fire our imaginations, we lift ourselves like the box kite out of our limitations and begin to move in a new direction, delightfully moving into a healthy future.

Ocean water moving in waves toward the beach captures our eyes and minds. The warmth of the sun nudges nimbly over our shoulders, as it glistens on the incoming waves. When we sit next to a wonderful new person we begin to dream of a perfect future. In that moment, we all transcend time and are drawn into a future expectation that guides our lives in a new direction. We write poetry about those moments. We are as the ocean, moving with force and brightness. We feel uplifted. We dare, in those moments, to become more fully ourselves. However, if the burgeoning love falters and is terminated, then we lose control and drift with deep longing and disorientation. The driving force that had engaged our attention and our energy no longer gives meaning to the future, and we slide into regret. It is the same way with our creative selves. When we falter with our creativity, we lose control of the energies within us that direct us toward the future with joy and determination. We find direction when expectations and desire draw us into the future. When we disengage ourselves from the creative flow, we begin to float, like driftwood, hoping some beach will offer comfort and a place to rest. But life is about energy and desire and moving. So we must take up the torch and light our fires, by reaching into our own extraordinary oceans and renewing our creative journeys through consistent love of our individual expression.

As a kid, I always loved stories of space. I loved going to the Hayden Planetarium, in New York City, to see the stars as brilliant dots against a concave ceiling and to view the asteroids that shocked the earth so many years ago. Space had all the characteristics of a great adventure.

It provided a dream for the future that was compelling. At age eleven, I found it a wonderful idea to travel into space. I thought it would be great to travel to the moon and so, right there among the circulating planets and eerie hallways, I signed up for the first voyages to the moon. As a result of that dream, I compiled my own loose-leaf book of hand-drawn constellations; I watched *Star Trek* and joined the British Astronomical Association to receive a journal with complicated mathematical formulas and data that left me clueless. But I was in love—I was uplifted from my mundane world to a hope for the future that could change my life's direction. I would need to go to college to read the symbols and understand the math. So when my father died suddenly, I had a mission to fulfill: a voyage to the moon! Looking back now, I might find it silly, but it does not matter what age we are, we need to maintain the wonder. We need to have a compelling dream to drive us into the future "where no one has gone before," because it is that very dream that keeps us alive, healthy, and creatively on the edge. To stop dreaming is to stop the imaginative flow of life's basic nature to create. The fire and the flow must remain within the constellations of your mind.

Our states of mind are precious indicators as to the course we are on for our future health and success. Often people find themselves without direction and completely convinced that they are doing all they can to derive the most from life. As we age, many of us tend to believe we have come up with the best ideas with which to run our lives. Or we may have become so burdened with the errors of the past that we are convinced of our inability to transcend our falls from grace. The problem with both points of view is that they speak of our immediate situations and not of the wonders that could be there in the future. The greatest thing about a dog is that it loves us with abandon. If we could only love ourselves in the same way, we could overcome our propensity for honoring our limitations. The dream of space, of going to the moon, of drawing a new reality is always within our grasp, but only if we see it.

We yearn for stability and concreteness: love that is unchanging, a future that we can count on, a financial environment that continues to grow. But stability and concreteness leave us in a world that is ever-changing and hard to control, no matter what we try. In our desire to stabilize we become more and more rigid in our behavior and thoughts—afraid of making a mistake and afraid of going in the wrong direction.

I remember when I was a baby; I had a crib that was made of metal. When I would touch the square rods that surrounded me, they were cold. This iron rectangular crib was stable and it imprisoned. Eventually, I was able to climb over the top, get to the floor, and peek through the door of the bedroom into the adult world. It took a lot of trial and error before I successfully overcame my restrictions. Looking back, I am sure my parents weren't as happy as I was with my newly won freedom.

I find myself, at times, revisiting that crib with its coldness and rust-colored rods. I wonder if perhaps I am still encompassed by that container; am I restricted by my own thoughts and behaviors? In our attempt to control as much as possible in our lives, we sometimes become inflexible in our thinking and actions. We cautiously reenact what we have always done out of fear of failure, or losing nerve, or appearing foolish. Creativity grows out of flexibility, out of spontaneity and diversity of thought. But we often drop ourselves back into the iron crib. We become comfortable there, because it allows for the usual routine. So many of our actions come out of an established pattern of doing things, which in some cases is a good thing. When we drive a car or open a door, it is good that we do not need to review how to do it. However, when it comes to thinking more creatively, if we do not learn how to reach our legs up and over the bars of the crib, we will remain confined to our usual tracks of thought. To discover a different approach, to think different thoughts, we need to open our minds to our creativeness and not succumb to the iron rigidity of our usual patterns. It is easy to be logical, to stay practical, to control flights of fancy, but at what cost? The Nobel Prize winner Albert Szent-Gyorgyi said "Discovery consists of looking at the same thing as everyone else and thinking something different." How do you do that? By climbing out of the safety crib and taking a foothold in the creativity mountain of random and playful thinking. When you are under pressure, this might be difficult to do.

I recall being asked during "Show and Tell" in my kindergarten class to present something. I could not think of a thing. My friend, Jeffery, whose sister was having a birthday in a couple of days, gave me a birthday candle from his packet just before it was my turn to go up. I have no idea why I accepted his lone candle, as I reluctantly edged my way to the front of the class (in my short britches, which I hated). The heat in my face rose, as I desperately pressed the pink candle between my thumb and index finger. At the front of the class, I lost total control of my mind, and I stammered, "He gave it to me," pointing to Jeffrey, and immediately rushed back to my seat, red-faced and breathing hard—an experience that is still etched in my mind as if I'd been branded. It could easily have led to an abiding hesitation to speak in front of a group of people. But that would have kept me in the crib. Although I recognized my fear of speaking in front of people, I regularly brought myself before groups by becoming a teacher. It was extremely difficult at first. In time, however, it got better, and I no longer experience internal tremors as I present my material.

The candle, however, lingered for a long time as a symbol of momentary incompetence. As confidence in my creative self emerged, I came to enjoy speaking with spontaneity. My more rigid thought patterns faded, and I was able to make different connection between things. The candle then changed and came to symbolize Jeffrey's friendship—a unity that was meant to overcome the immediate difficulties and challenges of life. If only I could have thought of that in Miss Price's kindergarten class, I probably would not have had so many years of stage fright.

Conquering your greatest fears can bring you to your greatest rewards. It is the trial by fire. It is the melting of your old confining ways and molding them into something new and personally rewarding. How often do we hold ourselves back from the very things we would like to do as a result of some anxiety or fear? As Tony Robbins so ably puts it at a workshop I attended, "The past does not equal the future." We always can have the ingenuity and the innovation necessary to develop a new future for ourselves that can be more engaging and interesting than the experiences of our past. It takes imagination and creativity. It takes overcoming the ironclad crib of our restrictive thinking and replacing it with the playful creativeness that each of us has within. We need to unwrap the swaddling and expose the creativity.

Iron is the sixth most common element. It needs to be melted out from its natural state and refined to become something that we can use. Fire has the power to refine and liquefy, to produce new from old. The beauty of a fire never ceases to mesmerize the young or the old. A huge bonfire can cause whole groups of people to congregate, stare, and throw another log on the fire, sending sparks flying up into the black night rich with stars. Crackling hot wood adding to the fun and the aroma of this event speaks to us on levels that are both ancient and universal. Our heavens swirl with fire lights and beauty and the ashes of time gone. From this rich array we can build our stories. We can play with our imaginations to construct myths and songs. We can draw and paint. We can express from our own ashes and natural states the journey that we have taken in this life. To believe that we have nothing to say is to miss ourselves. We are as the universe—a mixture of light and darkness, of fire and iron. We have within us the power of the universe. We need to unlock the forces within, so that we can lead creatively fulfilling lives, not ones that monotonously move from day to day with perfect precision. Sometimes we want things to be so perfect that we engulf our time in meaningless repetition. The trouble with perfection is that it sometimes keeps us from finishing the things we want to do. These things can remain "not quite right" forever. We think that perhaps, with one more rewrite, or one more day or week of reviewing things, the project can become perfect. However, for most people, perfection is elusive and sadly handicapping. As you view the leaves of a tree on a sunny day, would you say that one leaf was less perfect than the others? Or would you instead admire the beauty of its lined expression of veins, colors, and branches?

It is important to recognize the function of fire and iron, to realize that as we age we become bound to the opinions, ideas, and behaviors that keep us in our cribs of restrictive patterns, and that only the fire of difficult times and fearful steps can bring us to an awakening of the beauty of ourselves and the strength that we possess as creative individuals. Jim Rohn, a famous lecturer and writer, said, in his book *7 Strategies for Wealth and Happiness*, "Don't wish for things to be easier, wish that you were better." It's true. Risk the disappointments, so that you can get better. Risk failure, so that you can learn how to succeed. Risk loving another, so that you can have a chance at being loved in return. Risk exploring your creativeness, so that you can join in the ancient rituals. Sit about the fire and tell your story, so that you can bring yourself to health and the joy of personal expression.

Early morning beauty

Striking the Match

Keep your journal by your bed, so that when you wake you can record your dreams. Dreams seem to slip away so quickly. It is good to catch them as soon as you can. If nothing else, recording them gives you another piece of your mental life, and it may give you transformative clues into yourself.

Buy a kite, and again experience the fun of constructing it and putting it up. It is sometimes easy and sometimes a struggle, but it offers a way back to the spontaneous joys of childhood when imagination was flying high. As you get older, it is so important to hang on to a thread of creativity and high-flying enthusiasm!

Find a painter whose work you love, and review each of his or her paintings. Discover new things within the painting that you might have missed before. Reflect on what led this person to choose this particular subject matter. How does it inform you? What emotions or thoughts are provoked by the painting? If you do not have at least one favorite painter, find one.

CONFUSION
Chapter Four

The frustration of "misplacing" our keys plagues most of us at one time or another. How do they get to be missing? Have we just mislaid them, or have we lost the memory of where we put them? It seems that the angrier we get about this situation, the harder it is to find the keys. When we do find them, we are amazed at where we left them. Not knowing where something is, or what something is about, can be frustrating and upsetting. As a result of this experience of loss and not knowing, we may select a particular place to regularly put the keys, so we do not go through the aggravation again. In our lives, we assemble things so that we can find them easily. We try to provide an order to things so that we can count on the way something will unfold. But we all know situations that did not unfold the way we thought they would. Relationships go in all kinds of crazy directions, especially if they are romantic. Many times we are left confused and dismayed. However, the situations that bring about confusion and disruption are the ones that teach us. They bring us to another level of understanding and knowledge.

It is interesting how often we try to hide and run from confusion, yet it is a vital part of the construction of something new. As much as knowing something allows you to build and make connections, so that you can think with more sophistication (such as algebra leading to calculus), it can also prevent you from learning something new, because you are so opinionated by what you know. As I see it, life is a continuing process of confusion, understanding, and knowing, confusion, understanding, and knowing, etc. It seems that we often try to avoid the confusion stage by constructing a view of the world that helps us avoid mistakes, discouragement, disorder, and failure. And then, when this stage does come, we ask why it had to be that way. Why are the keys missing? Why did he/she leave me? Why wasn't I promoted? In confusion, we search for answers that go beyond previous knowledge and previous expectations. It is not the time for self-flagellation, but a time for renewal, for reconstruction—for seeing beyond the chaos of the moment and joining the adventure of newness and entering into a creative flow.

A few years ago, I wandered into the Picasso Museum in Paris. It was a rainy day, the cobbled streets were slick, and the red flag of the museum was reflected distortedly in loose puddles. I always found the figures in Picasso's later paintings strange and disturbing, as if they came from a different space and time, ancient and foreboding. They stood out in all their distinctive difference, through sharp lines and discombobulated figures, to confuse and disorient the viewer. As I drifted from one room to the next, I realized that I was suddenly enchanted by the bulls, the horses, and the women. In the chaos of it all, I saw passion and pain. I saw the tangle and resolve of another man's view—with all its boldness, sorrow, anxiety, and love. It was an unusual afternoon, during which the old responses did not maintain themselves. I felt I was seeing something about myself that I had never seen before: a hidden passion, a sexual drive, a wonder that had slipped my attention before. In our lives, we must be grateful for those moments of illumination that suddenly reach out and embrace us. Many times those moments are accidental and disorganized. It is up to us to see them and take note of them.

As I was about to leave the museum, I decided to go up a "down" staircase. In the landing above, I saw Picasso's actual painting chair encased behind glass, as it peeked out in humble isolation. Without thinking, and with the people coming down annoyed and grumbling, I photographed that chair. If I hadn't had my camera, I would have missed it. If I hadn't gone up the down staircase, I would have missed it. If I was sane, I would have missed it. However, I got it. In the wildness of a moment, I allowed myself to feel and be—without hesitation, without the confines of logic—and to just spontaneously accept the chaos of it all, including the displaced eyes and cheeks. I wandered without expectations, without the usual confining thoughts that regularly kept me to my old routines, and, instead, jumped into the moment. His chair is a wonderful symbol of disarray, with paintbrushes willy-nilly in and out of the can resting on the seat; with paint drippings adding character and color to this random chair that became an important placement by the easel, close to the hand of Picasso. In other households it would have become garbage, but here it was under glass amongst the greatest of art. I could see in that chair all the artifacts that have ever been uncovered by archeologists and the joy that they must have felt with each additional find from their digs. It was as precious an object as one that actually had been in the hands of Queen Cleopatra. It defied time and added to the mystery of the man who originally used it.

Too often we miss what is around us, something that might add dimension to our lives, because our fixation is on order and not on the creative part of us that is open to explore and experience. I realize that if I hadn't taken a chance on a rainy day to explore and leave myself open to whatever happened I would never have accidentally found the museum or opened the doors to a greater insight into myself and to the joy of understanding archeological discoveries. We expand in our vision, as we allow ourselves to be open to the chaos that exists just beyond the doors of our controlled lives. Our joys can come from unexpected events and experiences.

The joy of a child being born into your life is a most beautiful and exciting experience. We usually do not know how we are going to raise this child or how he or she will alter our lives, but we are willing to take the risk. As the child grows, we realize not only the importance of having had the child but the significance the child has on our own lives and thoughts. Although we are quick to recognize and applaud a child born to us, we are reluctant to honor the child within us. It is creativity that nurtures and supports the child within us. We cannot neglect or shun it. When we do, life becomes repetitive and boring, leaving us regularly to discover a new diversion or activity to control our restless dissatisfaction. Divorce might work, as might changing jobs or having an affair. But the basic discontent will not be abated. We are an expressive people. Our inner children cry out for expression. They want to feel the comfort of a quiet stream, the touching of warm black dirt, the sweet aroma of flowers and weeds. Our children want to draw on walls, write dirty words, sing to the sun, jump rope, and see themselves reflected in a bountiful pond. Jumping on the back of a bus used to be an adventure; now it is a distance memory, as we wonder what happened to the time. The great thing about creativeness is that it is always young. It always speaks from the heart of a child. Nurture your child and accept the risk of not knowing and confusion. It will serve you well.

Sometimes we have memories of childhood that make more sense when we revisit them many years later than when they were fresh and kind of funny. One winter, my mother bought me this very handsome coat, which had an English plaid pattern to it and six rather large buttons. It was a very warm coat, and with gloves, which I hated, I could withstand any storm. My friend Martin had an old sled that, unfortunately, had a nail sticking up where you belly flopped in order to sled down this wonderfully steep hill by his house. After we had had a joyous time in the snow with the sled, it was time for us to come in and eat something. I did not see the huge rip until we were walking through the back door of his house. My mother was so upset with this L-shaped rip in my new coat that I have never forgotten her pained expression or the incident. For a time, I thought it was very funny. Being six at the time, I never realized why it was such a monumental event. However, with the passage of years I have realized that for my mother, who, along with my father, was struggling with finances, this was a disappointing and sad situation. The coat would never look as it was supposed to look, since it would forever have an L-shaped patch committed to its front. This memory, which spontaneously got recorded in my journal one day as I was reflecting on my life, gave me a sense of my mother that I might not have had if I had not recalled it. Her distress clearly showed the extent of her worries about trying to make ends meet, but since she did not punish me, she was showing me the extent of her love. Her conflict must have been tremendous, but her love for me exceeded her distress.

Since she died when I was twenty-two, it was good to have this memory resurrect itself in my journal when I was fifty.

There are people who feel that it is best to leave the child behind when you become of age. They feel that the naiveté and boundless scattered energy of childhood is not proper for the mature individual. It is interesting, however, that those who have aged with their child part still intact are more engaging, lively, and future oriented than those who have not. Such was the case with Frederick Franck, an internationally famous artist and writer who I visited a number of years ago. I went to meet Frederick Franck and his wife at their home in Warwick, New York, when he was ninety. I had been taking some of my workshop classes to do photography at his beautiful sculpture park and sanctuary called Pacem in Terris, which was part of his property. I had decided that I wanted to get his opinion on some of the photographs I had done there. As I waited in their rather small living room for him to come down some old wooden steps that I was facing, I was struck by the quiet darkness of the place. I remember feeling that I had drifted back to the turn of the twentieth century and was actually waiting for a local farmer. Perhaps it was the wooden table and chairs that gave me this impression, or the artifacts that were contained on shelves and window ledges. The adjacent kitchen looked cluttered and well used.

After his wife helped him carefully down the stairs, his stooped figure was overshadowed by a charming smile that greeted me with warmth and friendship. I had come on an impulse. I had called only two weeks before to see if it was possible to meet the man who had written *The Zen of Seeing*. This is a wonderful book about how to see more clearly what is before you, which I have recommended in my workshops. As we talked his age disappeared, and a liveliness became present that spoke with a richness of wonder, energy, and experience. He spoke of projects and art and the delight of having people visit his property. His wife's closeness to him and love were inspiring. There was simple magic before me in this small house next to a stream. It was the magic of passion and the child's ability to question and remain happily engaged. It was the magic of individual expression that only dies if we do not pay attention to the primary urges within us, which are to love and create. A good storyteller creates. A good cook creates. A good lover creates. When you stop the flow of your creativity, you bind yourself to an emptiness and loneliness that robs you of health and life itself. At ninety, Frederick Franck showed the power of the creative spirit that is within each of us as long as we find it and express it.

As we went through the different photographs I had taken, we got to one that I was particularly curious about, since I had felt so drawn to it when I originally took it. It was a large, black can, oddly shaped, that was being used for extinguishing cigarette butts. The photographs I was showing were all mounted on photo boards and approximately twenty by twenty-four inches in size. The black can in the photograph was about the same size as it was in real life. Frederick smiled at the image when I asked him what it was. I had told him how much I was attracted to the can and wondered what the story was behind it. He told me that he had bought some property in Holland, and when they had cleared part of the land, they had found this large can. It was an old milk can, which he thought dated back to the sixteen hundreds. What we are attracted to is always interesting!

Over the years, I have found myself attracted to farm life and the symbolism implied by the images of that life—stability, community, earth, food—the basic, and the primitive. One of my favorite short poems is William Carlos Williams' "The Red Wheelbarrow," which begins: "So much depends ..." And now I had my own short photographic poem representing all the intriguing ideas of the farm captured in a single image: So much depends on a milk can. So much depends on your ability to reach out to the child within to foster the joy of imagination and playfulness. We can all be intrigued by a milk can, a key, or an artifact from our childhood.

I have been asked by many people in various workshops, "How can I become more creative?" "How can I be a photographer?" And my answer, even before I realized the total value of what I was saying, was "Make believe you are." I would say, "Since you have taken this workshop, you can proclaim to yourself and others that you are a creative being (or you are a photographer, or you are an artist)." We can become what we believe. We can become what we name ourselves. If you were a "real" photographer, you would step up and take the photographs. You would not stand far back from what you wanted to take a picture of. You would confidently come close, get involved, and push your way into the mix. You would gain access to the spot from which to take the best photograph. There will be boldness to you when you have named yourself. Creativity comes in abundance when you name yourself creative—when you lift the crayons, the pencils, the paints or the music sheets and draw or write as you have defined yourself. It is amazing how changing the title of yourself, and believing it, can alter your performance. In creative writing classes that I have run, there are people who will say that they would like to write, but they really can't write that well. The biggest block we put before ourselves is when we say that we cannot do something. As much as we hear about *self-fulfilling prophecy*, we continually neglect heeding its message. Our ideas and labels about ourselves will define us. We need to give ourselves good labels. We are a rich source of talent. Our minds have extraordinary potential, but, without exploring and reaching out, we remain humbly unnamed, drawing in lack of confidence and expectations. Without pressure, we need to name ourselves and then regularly perform the tasks of that title. If it is writing, we must write. If it is painting, we must paint. If it is music, we must play. We must practice our art without words of *lack*, without *can't*, and play in the playground of children, where the key words are: "Do you want to play cowboys and Indians?" "Do you want to play creative?"

The journey to a more creative life is within your grasp. Approach it with openness and a sense of adventure. So many people are afraid of confusion and failure. But you cannot allow these thoughts to interfere with something that can heighten your awareness, improve your lifestyle, expand your horizons, and offer you a healthier and more engaging life. When you seek creative expression, you release yourself from the usual bonds that control your life. The bonds may be: *follow the rules, find the "right" answers, be practical, avoid ambiguity,* and *don't play—work.* These bonds all seem logical until you realize that none of these strategies have gotten you to where you would like to go creatively. If anything, they prevent you from engaging in the creative process. If you follow the rules, you may function merely by rote and feel bored and unable to understand how the rules apply to what you are doing. With the restrictions of rules, you may become dissatisfied and give up, losing a valuable connection to self. Giving yourself over to confusion and openness, you may not find the "right" answer. Instead, you may find many answers—each one interesting in itself, and, therefore, giving you another way of seeing things. To be practical would mean that your creative expression would have to take second place to just about everything else, since creativity is never characterized as a practical endeavor. Play, after a certain age, seems frivolous and only for those who have not really grown up to become part of the adult world. They are the strollers of life who cannot seem to grasp the importance of mature living. And, finally, we have the word that causes horror to many people: ambiguity. It has a disconcerting ring to it that unnerves the more practically minded adult. We become victims of our language. We become trapped by the words that we utter to ourselves on a regular basis. To overcome this, we need to embrace ambiguity and chaos. We should enjoy our random thoughts of fantasy and escape, indulge ourselves in the mystery of the vaulted mind, and explore what is not known and what is not obvious or definable in logical equations.

To explore and develop our creativity, we need the pleasure of walking unencumbered by the negative postures of our minds. Thoughts of failure or not enough time ("I'll do it later") need to be deleted from our minds. Brief moments each day devoted to our individual expression will give us an accumulation of material that we will become excited about. As our creative expressions begin to accumulate, our attraction for them will increase, and our feelings of accomplishment will also mount.

I remember one day deciding that I would blow up a photograph or two from one of the weddings that I had shot. I had been a professional photographer for a while, and there were some images that I particularly liked. I am not sure what possessed me to choose the shot I did, except that it had some meaning to me that went beyond what was obvious at the moment. I just wanted one really big picture. It was a photograph of a small bridal party walking across the lawn of New Rochelle College. The reason I chose this shot was that there, in the bridal party, was an eleven-year-old boy who looked so pained in his black tuxedo and crooked bow tie that he had become, for me, the quintessential kid inflexibly bound to a situation he did not want to be in. Nothing could be worse on a hot, boring day than to walk across a wide field, with drooping shoulders and cranky legs, marching with your aunt's wedding party. It was priceless. I had taken this image long before journalistic wedding photography was even thought of as an alternative to the formal style. The blow-up that I made was thirty by forty inches. It has received many wonderful comments over the years. But there's more to it than that. This single large image impressed me so that I decided to enlarge other images. Something happened when I made them really big. I saw my work more as art than just candid photographs. They had a life to them that challenged my interest and my desire. I wanted to have more images that looked like art. I began shooting photographs to see how I could use camera angles, lighting, and subject matter to create more artfully done images. What started out as one enlarged image became a whole collection of images. People liked the little images, but they loved the bigger ones more. This enlarged collection of photographs later became a showcase for teaching people photography.

We can never tell where things will lead before we start. It is the starting in the mess of things that makes the biggest difference. I worked at a bar in Queens for a couple of years during the morning and early afternoon shift. Every day, Johnny, a man in his late twenties, would come in for his usual and talk about how he was going to take some courses to be a plumber so he could quit working as a garbage man. He told me this regularly, with sincerity, until the day I left, two and a half years later. He never started. To never start is indeed a shame.

As time has passed, I have wondered about what meaning there could be to spontaneous thoughtless expression. Although it may seem strange, I have concluded that we are always guided by some force that is deep within us. At times, we can glimpse at the connections between things, but many times they remain hidden. This is one of the reasons creative expression is so important in our personal development. It provides us with signs and indications as to what direction we should go—to renew ourselves and shed old postulates for new ones that will give meaning to our days and experiences. At our centers, we all have the desire to know the meaning of things. Sometimes we desire to reach from the ashes of our lives to something that will transform us and our lives or that will maintain and support the life we have lived with the vigor and interest that we have enjoyed so far. Whatever the case, we seek to discover a wellspring of new meaning and wonder, so that our journey does not become staged and boring.

I have often wondered what meaning this big picture of a boy in a wedding party has for me that makes me keep it through the years and transport it from one home to another, like a child's favorite doll or tattered blanket. The march from church to reception across an empty field was significant to me in what way? In the boy I saw the frustration of containment, while he crossed a field in which he could break free and run and gambol. The rigidity of the tuxedo prevented immediate escape. In his walk there was the message that his discontent was great and that at some point he would have to be released from this formal attire. I saw in him a piece of myself—that part that wants to break free from the restrictions of life, to run from the demands of order to experience the freedom of the random field, and to overcome the limitations of time and place. I also saw the happiness of the bride and groom alongside the boy and realized our struggle to maintain our individual selves in the midst of coupling. I saw the tension that is created within us between the selfish and the unselfish, between the *me* and the *you*. It was interesting to see all the thoughts that came up when I reflected on this big picture. The mind sees many things at the same time. What do you see in your "big picture" that you have carried over the years either in your mind or in a frame?

Striking the Match

Find an image that expresses a way of life to you. Is it a particular building in the midst of a big city, or a cottage tucked away between tall trees? When you find it, you will know. Write about this image, and explore what it means to you. How we see things defines us. Seek to discover your definitions of self.

Interview an artist about his or her work. They are always around. Outdoor or indoor exhibits are always good places to meet artists. Sometimes they come and talk at local libraries or bookstores. Take advantage of the opportunity to explore with live dialogue what motivates him or her.

Begin to collect images of things or people that you like. Get posters or other things from museums, galleries, or bookstores, so that you can surround yourself with inspirational objects. Even postcards of your favorite painters can be a wonderful addition to your "imaginings."

THE POWER OF YOUR MIND
Chapter Five

We can travel anywhere we want through the power of our minds. Even as I sit before this computer, I can see myself back in Paris at the Park Hotel, with a lovely young woman speaking French at the reception desk in front of me. The couch I am sitting on is of a pale peach. The single TV on my left is a little too loud for me to hear what is being said at the desk. I am waiting for my friend, who is still in our room getting dressed. The daylight coming in behind me is from a tiny courtyard with greenery and closely packed walls. Outside, through the automatic doors, is St Michel running along the Seine with the Norte Dame Cathedral in the background to the right. I am amazed at how well I can bring back this delightful experience to my mind. It is not totally perfect, since I am really not there, but I am close enough to regain the experience with an authenticity that brings me so very close to it. This is the true wonder and power of our minds, the ability to re-experience the details of a distant experience, to recognize a vast variety of objects, and to learn. We are blessed with great powers.

When you consider what you can create, you realize that you have amazing resources. Your mind has everything that you need to overcome any pressing momentary conflicts or uncertainties. This is certainly true when we reach a point in life where we do not know how to precede or get beyond where we are. These feelings of uncertainty come to us whether we are young or old. Life takes turns that we were not expecting, and suddenly we are at some crisis point and not sure how to move forward. In these moments, these new beginnings, we tend to drift through the days hoping that something will change, some miracle will occur, and everything will return to order again, with our sense of balance regained. It is during these times when we're not sure what's next that our creative selves are so important, since they have the power to lead us in a positive and rewarding direction. You should realize that our minds are a mystery that requires our attention and admiration. Our lack of focus and attention will undermine our potential, leaving us with less than we could have gotten. Therefore, our energy should be used to direct our minds, to use the richness and power to expand our vision and our lives, and to encourage our creative selves. Let this focus bring you back to old memories and places so that you can savor the re-experience and learn as it unfolds again. In our past are the secrets that will fulfill our present.

As an example, I remember a house that I wanted to rent with a friend of mine in Nyack, New York. It was across a narrow street that faced the Hudson River. It stood on a slight hill with well-tended grass and a couple of trees that reached above the lower floors to give shade during hot summer days to its wide porch. This porch that faced the Hudson had two wooden rocking chairs with flattened hand-made pillows on them. After my friend and I had viewed the house, we sat on the chairs rocking for a while, as we discussed the rental and how we could pay for it. The house had attracted us because of its winding staircases and rooms that seemed casually spread about in a random manner. There were secret closets and tiny hiding places that would make any child cry out with glee. Having grown up in an apartment, I had never seen a house that had such a child's sense of imagination to it. It reminded me of the tunnels and tents I used to construct when I was a kid to make the simplest surroundings into an adventurous environment. Secret hiding places had always been a must.

The house had such charm, with its intricate passageways and two large fireplaces that were perfect for toasting marshmallows or for staring into the dancing flames. It was a place that encouraged reflection. It was a place of childhood imagination and of safety, so that you could release the reveries of your mind.

Although we ended up not renting this place, I have always been glad that we had the experience of it. We all need a place where we can reflect in peace and safety, even if it is an imagined revisitation. There are times I have rocked on that porch again and enjoyed the evening sun turning the river into shining bits of orange. It is important to have a place that brings us a sense of peace. Even if it is imagined, it has tremendous power. We learn from our reveries and imagined returns. It is within this scope that we discover ourselves and what we most want. Each of us needs to find a place where we can be ourselves and do the things that will help us grow. In Edward Albee's play *A Delicate Balance,* Tobias, upon being offered the possibility of a new life on a far-off island, absently says, "It's … it's too late, or something." Don't let that be your answer. It is never too late to find the place or to unlock the mind's secret rooms. It is so important to reflect and discover the hidden treasures of your being.

The power of our experiences is always there for us to explore. Our minds always have the ability to organize, to make connections, to jump tracks, and to wildly create. There is a profound river that runs through each of us, which contains the uniqueness of our being. All we need to do is to regularly take notice of it and discipline ourselves to express it. Without discipline, our minds wander and spin through the flotsam of our lives. The easiest way to lose ourselves is to stay thoughtfully stuck on whatever our minds want—which is usually to go through all that did not work: relationships, business, investments, etc. My suggestion is to override the connection. Our joy comes through renewal and expression, through activity and reflection. It is our reliance on routine that holds us to old patterns and prevents our internal power from exhibiting itself. Whatever we do not use becomes dormant and requires even more energy and discipline to awaken. Activity and practice keep the spirit moving and give our forlorn parts new life.

To reach for and expose your creative power, it is necessary to practice thinking beyond the usual, the logical, the comfortable, and the reliable. It is daring something that you never thought you would dare to do. It can be as silly as eating chocolate ice cream everyday for a whole week so that the kid in you is truly awakened in gleeful completeness. You never know how freeing it can be to be a child again until you try it. In a lovely short essay, Nadine Stair says, "If I had my life to live over, I would start barefoot earlier in the spring and stay that way later in the fall. I would go to more dances. I would ride more merry-go-rounds. I would pick more daisies." Sometimes we get so caught up in the struggles of life that we forget the simple joys that are around us, which can help us see the beauty and wonder of our world.

I have always loved merry-go-rounds. There was one in Central Park in New York City that had a delightful CLANG, CLANG just before it started; this set my heart to pounding, as the brilliant horses began to move, and the mechanical organ festively played. If you close your eyes, I am sure you can hear the music. The more you hear the music, the more you can see and feel the swirling up-and-down movements of the carousel. It was so exciting. I hated to get off. I loved waving to my mom and then to my dad, and then to my mom, and then to my dad, as it turned around and around, never catching up to the horse in front. I was annoyed sometimes that the horses were stationary and I could not gallop just a bit faster so I could pass the first horse. But, alas, it would not break free and overcome the steed in front. Creativity peeks out from behind painted horses and mounds of ice cream. Varying your routine and engaging your senses will always refresh your sometimes-routine life. It is like lighting a sparkler on the Fourth of July.

To have your creativity blossom takes practice and a desire to have it become a key part of you. Your creativeness will remain dormant until you awaken it. Creativity requires acknowledgement and practice. Muscles grow with use and exercise; you can strain them to go beyond the point they were at before. The value is in the feeling, in the sense of renewed and expanded strength that you have as a result of regular practice. Too often we want things to happen without doing too much. We feel that wishing will make it get better over time. I would suggest not wishing. Use your muscles *today*. Stretch yourself today, so that tomorrow you can feel the power of your mind and your creativity.

Quite a few years ago, I felt in a rut. My job had gotten monotonous, and I received little or no sense of satisfaction from it, even though I had performed my job with dedication and enthusiasm. At that time, I was a high school English teacher. It was not my students that I was dissatisfied with; it was the system. The financial compensation was low; the work hours were long; the routine of the classes was unimaginative; and the recognition for teachers, who usually performed well, was very limited, if it existed at all. Most really good teachers I knew left to seek better-paying jobs in business, where their energy and performance would be rewarded.

In my desire to discover what to do with my life if I left high school, I enrolled in a workshop that dealt with something called neuro-linguistic programming, or NLP, for short. It was an interesting program that offered ways to help you understand the communication process as well as to reprogram behaviors you had that you would like to change. I went through many levels of the training, until I reached a point where I was training other people in the techniques and strategies of the program. The workshops provided many benefits to those who participated, and put into practice the information that was presented. As a result of going through this training, I left teaching and went into business for myself. It altered my life. It gave me a whole new direction that would never have happened if I had not ventured out into this workshop, into this something new.

Personal development is an ongoing experience. Reawakening your passion for living is essential for having a satisfying and creative life. Although you may not see the solution to a current problem, it is always there, as long as you search for it in new and different places. There is no doubt that remaining with the same thought patterns that you have always had will produce the usual results. It is only when you move in a new direction that you can alter your life, making it richer and more joyful. Using workshops or seminars to improve yourself is an excellent way to bring into your life the alternatives that can help you become all that you can be.

Our bodies require that we nourish them on a regular basis. When we get hungry, our bodies remind us with internal rumblings that it is time to eat. Some of us even get cranky as a result of our hunger. Since we have a number of different signs to help us continue to nourish our bodies, we maintain them on a regular basis. The problem with the mind is that it does not give us a sign to indicate that it needs nourishment. It seems willing to allow the same material to circulate through it—without saying a word to stop the regurgitation of old ideas and information. It may even seem contented with this recycled-thinking process, as if it were essential for maintaining and supporting the personality and character of those of us whose minds are in the groove. However, this kind of complacency with mental activity only prevents us from using a resource that has tremendous power to help us live happier, healthier, and more creative lives. Our minds need to refill and reexpand the reservoir with new and different information, so that new linkages between thoughts and actions can be made. We can always improve and expand our minds. It requires introducing ourselves to new material, new books, and new ideas to help us see things more dynamically, more imaginatively, and more insightfully. Some of us leave college never to absorb again the variations of knowledge that are regularly presented there. It is true that time changes things. We are no longer confined to one location. The world is at our fingertips. We can instantly, with our pocket "magic boxes," see what is happening in different parts of the world. However, our limitations are the same today as they were centuries ago. The limitation of any individual is the extent to which his or her knowledge and skills have been developed. You cannot fake your personal level of development. It manifests itself in everything that you do. Your behavior is dictated by the thoughts that you have learned to embrace and regularly reiterate. If you attempt to show a larger, grander picture of yourself, people will know, at some point, that it is fluff.

To me, cotton candy in pink always looked more joyful than the ones in blue; either way, I never liked cotton candy. The first time I had it, I was so excited, since it looked so good and big. How big was it? Really big! However, when I got this wonderful fluff in my hand, and peeled off a sticky piece of it, and stuck it into my mouth, I realized immediately that I had been misled. I had been taken for a ride. I no sooner got a large tasty piece of it into my mouth than it disappeared into a tiny spot of raw sugar and then was totally gone. I can still remember the shock I felt. If I had gotten a candy bar (not even a big one), it would have lasted five times longer than the cotton candy. We may want the process of training and educating ourselves to be shorter, but the focus must always be on the journey. If you want a life rich in beauty and happiness, then you need to do the things that will help you reach that level of experience. Fluff only lasts so long.

We can throw our bodies out into the world and do many different kinds of things, but if the activities do not fulfill our internal yearnings, we will always feel dissatisfied and want for something else. Our minds desire meaning and an experience that will satisfy that childish part of us that wants creative expression, knowledge, and fulfillment. There are so many self-help books, because the desire to find the answers and resolve our issues is ever present in us. It is only in learning to know ourselves, in taking that journey inward, that we begin to discover what most moves us intellectually, emotionally, and spiritually. In my experience, there are many ways of accomplishing this. One can be through simply drawing. It is amazing how a single quickly done drawing can clearly delineate our fondest dreams. And it is our dreams that keep us in good spirits.

Children are so happy when they express their dreams to us. This is like a light brightly illuminating the whole room. Our depression sometimes comes as a result of relinquishing our dreams, of denying our inner child, or of losing our resilience and enthusiasm for life. In an art therapy training program I was attending in New York City about ten years ago, I was given an assignment that required a single quick drawing of how I pictured my future life. Within the drawing, I was also to write down the specific things I wanted for my future personal and business life. Although I was clear on what was being asked, I could not quite get a handle on what to put down, and so I delayed doing the exercise until the morning of the next class. In a bit of a rush, I filled the drawing sheet with lines and trees and scribbles. It quickly unfolded with images and a list of specific spontaneous thoughts for the future. What is truly amazing is that this last-minute drawing has been an extraordinary representation of how my life has unfolded over the years since its flamboyant expression.

On some level I must have realized its power and purpose, because, not only did I hold on to it over the years, but I framed it, so I could hang it up and see it on a regular basis. Some of the things that were listed on this casual sheet were going to Paris, developing ongoing training programs, lecturing in distant places, having gallery exhibitions of my photography, growing in new and different ways, etc. Almost all of the listed items have entered my life over the ensuing years. What is surprising is that none of these things were part of my life at the time.

They just spontaneously came as I tried to finish this random picture. We need to appreciate and utilize this amazing power that is within us! Our creative minds know things that we do not know on a conscious level. Our unrest frequently comes from the fact that we are not in alignment with our internal knowing power, and we are not using this power to bring ourselves to a more rewarding and energizing level of being. Sometimes the briefest of exercises can bring the greatest of insights.

Although we may be afraid of wasting our time with childish activities, these very activities could give us insights into our lives that might not materialize in any other way. I have learned to be open to those momentary flashes of thoughts or images, which seem tangential but provide subtle clues as to what I need to do to make my life better or to solve problems that have been nagging and frustrating me. We are given to missing things, to being too familiar with the regular laying out of our days, and, therefore, being numbed to really "seeing" beyond the usual. If I had missed that drawing exercise, would things have unfolded as they did? It is hard to say, but I am grateful that it happened, since it gave me a focus and a looking-forward-to experience that I am sure helped me achieve those exposed subconscious goals. Reaching inside of ourselves is the only way to discover what we truly want in our lives as well as what we really have to offer. We must understand that the power we hold within us is truly amazing, and all we need to do is nurture and free it from its confinement.

It has long been known that we only use a very small part of our mental capacity. Even though many of us know this, we regularly deny that we could do more than we are doing. It seems that we feel too exhausted to spend another hour reading or studying for our self-improvement. We would like things to go quicker and with less effort. We have forgotten how long it took to learn to skateboard or play tennis or swim well. In some cases, we practiced these things as a result of real desire to do them well. However, when it comes to our own mental development, we seem to be less enthusiastic and disciplined. We may realize how important it is to lose weight and exercise, but we tend to allow time to slip past the moment for committing. This is also true of exercising and feeding our creative powers. We let things slip. We may feel an hour of drawing is a waste of time. Meditating for half an hour may not seem like time wisely used. We have so many things to do. Sitting and writing in our journals cannot help with paying the bills or fixing the faucet or going to the store. Practicing at the piano for an hour may not be on today's schedule. In order to grow, we need to indulge ourselves in the joys of self-improvement. We need to cultivate our powers, so that they do not drift away and leave us empty and wanting. We need to discipline ourselves to do the things that will improve us mentally, so that as we age we have enthusiasm, energy, and enterprise right up to our final days. Without these things, we merely drift in aimless frustration. Drifting is very easy. One day very quietly slips into another, and before you realize what has happened, a day becomes a week, a week becomes a year, and a single year becomes ten. It is so easy to drift. And your mind will let you do it, too. If you want more, you will need to *do* more.

At age fifteen, I became disenchanted with high school. I can see that day as clearly as if it were just last week. I was walking to school with a girl named Audrey. We had been going out for a month and a half. I had very cleverly gotten to sit next to her in my math class. This very pretty girl said to me as we were walking to school, "I don't want to date you anymore." Well, the world collapsed in that instant, and we just stopped and looked at each other for a few brief moments. I said, "I do not understand." Why I said that I have no idea. Nodding as strongly as I could under the circumstances, I mumbled, "It's been nice." And she said, "We can still be friends." I continued to nod and said, "Of course." And then I did something that surprised even me. I politely said that I had forgotten one of my books that I needed for class and turned around and went back home. I never went back to that school again. I do not know what happened to Audrey or the endless classes that I no longer attended. It was a stupid decision, and it definitely changed my life. When I look back, I realize that the only reason I went to class was to see her and ask her out, so it really was not her fault that I quit. I think we had about five or six dates.

After this experience, I realized that it was essential to fight for what you wanted and that it was silly to give up too soon. From age fifteen to nineteen I drifted, not knowing what I wanted to do or what I wanted from life, since I was basically on my own and living in the streets. It was a difficult period, filled with uncertainty and lack of direction.

Since I was underage and working at a bar, a job I hated, I soon learned that it was important to figure out what you wanted to do and then do everything in your power to accomplish it. However, it was easier to think about than it was to actually do. Life has some strange turns. One minute you are racing along going nowhere, and then suddenly something captures your attention.

For me, it was passing the New School of Social Research in New York City, as I was going to visit my mother's old friend, Mary, to have a cup of Earl Grey tea and some crackers. Mary's brother, Richard Connell, was a screenwriter, and he had had some stories published. So, over some English tea, I discussed with Mary how I would love to be a writer. In order to do this, I decided that I should enroll at the New School and take some writing classes. Mary thought it was a lovely idea.

From having no direction, I now had a college direction. For the next year and a half, I took a number of classes not only in writing but in political science and sociology. It was wonderful being a college student, even though I was still a high school dropout. Our minds have tremendous capacities. It is only when we allow ourselves to encourage and improve our minds that they will give us their richness and power. We will never know what we can accomplish if we do not extend ourselves and do what we might think is beyond us. Our creativeness is always within our reach. I could have remained a high school dropout and never considered college if it hadn't been for a decision to explore my creative side with writing. As a result of going to the New School, I met two wonderful writers who gave me the desire to develop my writing as well as my mind. Within the next year and a half, I had published one of my stories, and I had taken classes with Richard Yates, writer of *The Revolutionary Road,* and Hayes B. Jacobs, editor for the *Writer's Digest* magazine. I also went back to high school to get a diploma. We will never know what we can do until we venture out and use the power that is within each of us.

Duplicity

Striking the Match

Pick up a book today and read about art, about creativity, or about something you have always wondered about, whether it be anthropology, history, the Greeks, onions, language, music, etc. Reading is an imaginative experience. It allows your mind to create the pictures and to make the associations. Reading is a valuable way to expand your creativity.

Take a moment and write about an early romantic experience you have had. Review your reactions to it and what you learned from this experience. Sometimes mishaps teach us how to proceed in the future. Something in that we-can-still-be-friends comment might serve to expand your feelings and your creativity.

Think about what you find most enjoyable about life, and write a poem about it. Let it reflect your immediate responses. Take joy in its unfolding, no matter how silly and un-poemlike it might be. You are doing it for the fun of it.

Exploring New Routes
Chapter Six

The world is such a big place that you have to wonder why so many of us get stuck on one small speck of it, routinely cleaning, cooking, and staying. I remember reading William Henry Hudson's *Green Mansions* when I was a kid and getting lost in this magical jungle somewhere in South America. A beautiful nymph ran through the tangle of the underbrush and the tall trees with such great abandon that she was forever my heroine. The enchanted jungle was a natural wonder that attracted and mesmerized anyone who entered its fantastic world. To my young mind, Ruma represented the quintessential woman, with scant clothing and long, flowing black hair. I dreamed of the lush green of South America and of traveling up the Amazon River to find my imaginary lost love. But time passed without the exploration or the memory of this childhood fantasy, until I recently recalled the book and wondered what had happened to my profound desire to explore the South American jungles. Did I see it as an impossible journey or as an idle wish that had gotten swallowed with age and practical work experience?

So many dreams run through us that it is easy to neglect them and leave them to float unattended in some mentally distant river—to come back to us only in rare moments of discontent. Each of us needs to discover which dreams are essential to our being, so that we do not lose ourselves in the mix of multiplying days. Sometimes we dream too many things and then get lost deciding which one to focus on. Fortunately or unfortunately, our choices determine our lives. As Robert Frost so aptly put it, "Two roads diverged in a yellow wood … and I—I chose the one less traveled by." Our choices make all the difference. What road or roads have you chosen? Have your roads been leading you to where you want to go? If not, why not change them—now!

New roads may be confounding, upsetting, and even frightening. But they provide you with a new landscape, one that could alter how you see things. What I have found from working with many people is that it can be a lot easier than we first imagine. The new road does not have to be so difficult that you cannot bear to go through the experience of it. It can give you an experience that allows you to feel stronger and more confident within yourself. A few years ago, I was in Dallas staying with some friends of mine, when I decided to go to the movies to see a Japanese movie called *Ran*. My friends did not want to go, but they let me borrow their car. I ventured out with only a very rough idea as to where the movie theater was located and how I would get there. I drove to the theater in daylight, so I did not have too much trouble weaving through the city. The theater was old and had a great deal of charm and character that showed in the wonderfully carved decorations, the subdued lighting, and the aging regal drapes. It also had a bar as soon as you walked in the entrance, which surprised and delighted me. After a soothing gin and tonic, I indulged myself in a three-and-a-half hour movie that was both absorbing and visually exciting. I was so glad I had come to see it. The trouble began, however, after I entered the darkened area of the parking lot after the movie. As I looked out at the lot, I could not tell where I had parked the car. I was surprised at how big the parking area looked. It seemed unending. I literally had to wait until most of the people had driven away to discover that the car had not been stolen and that it was much further out of the way than I remembered. With great relief, I got in, started it up, and moved toward the exiting areas with the rest of the cars. Upon hitting the streets, I realized that I was not sure in which direction I needed to go. There was an initial moment of panic, as the bright lights and the fast-moving traffic interfered with my concentration. Finally, I began slowing my breathing down enough to decide what I should do. I knew my friends' names, but not their house address. I did not have their telephone number with me, nor was it even early enough to call, since it was about one o'clock in the morning. I began to look for anything that looked familiar, that could help me backtrack to their neighborhood and their house. It was such a strange experience. I had never been to this part of the city before, and I had not had a car to travel around with before. They had driven me to the workshop that I was attending each day and had picked me up at the airport when I arrived. In my lost state, I wondered what meaning this particular experience had for me. I was now aggravated, disturbed, and anxious. How the hell was I going to find my way back?

In our lives we enter times when we are truly lost and find ourselves going through many challenging emotions. All we want during this kind of situation is to fight free from the pain and discomfort of it and to ask someone to give us the right direction, so we can end our inner turmoil. In my case, I did not have enough information to even ask someone for help. Sometimes we have to figure it out for ourselves. We have to choose the best direction and route that we can come up with at that moment in our lives. We must use our internal strength and intuition, must use our creativeness to overcome the obstacles that we have encountered. I am not sure how my visual memory of the route was brought forth so that I could retravel it, backward, but after forty-five minutes or so, I drove into my friends' garage—much to my amazement. It may seem odd, but that experience gave me a greater sense of myself. I learned that I could trust myself when I was lost—that if I did not panic and could coolly consider the best things to do, I would regain my balance and find my destination. It was an important lesson. If I had not gone to see *Ran,* I could have missed a valuable experience by being unwilling to risk being lost. I have often wondered if I had not been lost in Dallas that night how my life might have been different. A single experience can alter our lives in such a way that we are never the same. We always seem to look for things to happen in a big way and, as a result, ignore the smaller, less dramatic things, as if they have little impact or importance. However, when we recall those moments later in our lives, many that had seemed only slightly significant when they occurred suddenly seem more meaningful. In looking back, we realize that those little moments were turning points, and our lives were changed as a result of those simple incidents. Paying attention to whatever happens in our lives is so important. And sometimes one experience leads into another without us even realizing its initial connection.

About four years after the Dallas experience, I went to Paris to teach an advanced program in photography. Since it was my first time flying to Paris, I decided I would go alone on a separate flight from the one the group was taking. It was a long flight and a bit boring, but I was excited about finally going to this dream place and teaching a group of my students there. Over the past few years, we had done a lot of photography together, traveling to different places to gain new perspectives and situations for our images. We had done many trips to Manhattan to photograph around Wall Street, and the South Street Seaport, and Central Park. We had traveled upstate to Woodstock, Sugarloaf, and Skyline Park. We went into forests, streams, old barns, wooden covered bridges, and ice cream parlors—all to capture that one great shot that we could prize, enlarge, and hang on the wall with our signature brazenly showing in the corner of the image. We had photographed horses, children, buildings, birds, flowers, cats, watering cans, alleyways, and whatever crossed our paths! Since we had gone to many places within a fifty-mile range of my studio, we were looking for a new location that would offer us a new adventure. Some had said the Virgin Islands, and I had said, "Why not Paris?" The romance of it charmed some, but others felt it was too far and, perhaps, too expensive. However, when the costs were calculated and the decisions were made, we concluded that Paris fulfilled more of our dreams than the Virgin Islands. It was a splendid decision for many reasons. In the end, we all gained experiences that we would never forget, and, at the same time, we took fantastic photographs.

It was a crisp, brilliantly sunny day when my plane landed at de Gaulle International Airport. After going through customs and getting out into the total bustle of the airport, I realized that I did not know how I was going to get to my destination, since I did not speak French, did not have a guide book, did not hear anyone speaking English, and, worse, there were serious, uniformed men walking about with automatic weapons. It was so strange being in a situation where you could not communicate and felt very uncomfortable. As I wandered about, trying to decide who I could ask or what I should do, I decided that I would ask whoever came the closest to me accidentally. A balding, middle-aged man who was coming out of an elevator paused not too far from me. I immediately jumped at the opportunity. He politely told me where the bus was that would take me to the metro, so I could go to the center of the city where I had lodging. I had lucked out in meeting one person who could speak English.

The bus was free, thank God. But the metro was not. I struggled to figure out what I needed to get into the metro. Anyone I approached told me they only spoke French. And everyone had picture cards that went into a machine that allowed them to go through. I just stood on the sidelines, trying to look as composed as I could, hiding my frustration and confusion. As I walked about, I saw a window where tickets were being purchased. The woman behind the counter did not speak English and kept asking me questions that I could not answer. The people behind me moved to one of the other lines, as I struggled to understand what she was asking me. She finally took my dollars, gave me francs and a ticket, and pointed to one of the gates that I imagined I needed to go through.

The station was slightly below ground and had wonderfully decorated billboards. The sunlight still slipped through some of the overhead openings to give a warm glowing light to this part of the platform. A train finally came, with a destination listed that matched the e-mail directions I had received from the hotel. Only a few people got on with me, and then off we went. I looked at a train station locator map encased in plastic on the wall inside. It looked as if I was heading in the right direction, and my stop was clearly listed on the map. I stared out at the graffiti, the backs of houses and buildings, the run-down lots, and the quickly passing stations. I checked the map four or five times just to make sure I had not missed my stop. We came to a stop, quite a few stations before mine, and everyone got off. I looked at the map and the empty compartment and wondered what I was missing. Then some people came on, and the doors shut. Although I thought I was fine, I wasn't. The train was going back in the direction from which it had just come. I was stunned. I reviewed the map and tried to speak to a few of the people, but I was alone with my useless American tongue. I then thought that maybe it needed to go back a little bit before it came forward again on another track. Wrong. I ended up back at the airport again. And I again saw a lovely billboard with Madonna on it. It is funny how the mind accepts and values the familiar. Although I was back where I had started, there was a feeling of safety. At least I knew this route. The challenge was what I would do when I got back to the last stop, which was not supposed to be the last stop!

As the train sped over the same tracks, showing the same windows and doors and graffiti, I carefully reviewed the map, trying to discover something that I had missed. But even with the whole trip back providing me time to review, I was as lost as before. This time I was getting off with all the others!

To be lost in a geographical location is very different from being lost within yourself. Both need, however, flexibility and resourcefulness, so that you can find your way. A cheerful smile helps as well. I moved with the throng in the hope I would discover someone speaking English. There were so many people in the underground station that at least it seemed reasonable. Finally I heard a man and a woman talking rather loudly in English. I rushed over, explained where I needed to go, and asked whether they could help me. Without actually stopping, they told me the metro number and approximately where it was. They then proceeded through the turnstile that required the little card to be inserted, where it would slip speedily through the machine and be retrieved on the other side of the turnstile. I quickly got mine out, but missed inserting it correctly and again had people moving over to the next line so they could avoid my jam-up. After I made several tries, it zipped through and patiently waited for me on the other side. However, my American friends were totally gone, and there was one tunnel leading to another tunnel leading to another tunnel until it seemed that I was worse off than before. The lost feeling compounded itself in this place. But I persisted. I moved forward. Watching the signs, adjusting my suitcase, and resolutely searching for the right platform. I passed a young man playing the sax, and a little further on, another playing guitar and singing. I wished I could stop, but I continued to scramble with the crowd through the tunnels. As much as I wanted to listen and join the fun of the underground, I was not sure of the outcome of this experience, although I did have the name and number of the hotel. Finally, the right sign with the right number appeared, and

I was again descending to yet another even lower level of this labyrinth of tunnels. At the crest of an escalator that descended even further, I saw my two acquaintances waiting for the train, still blabbing away without any regrets about leaving me. I felt no compunction to inform them that I had made it. We got on separate cars.

I again looked at the map behind plastic, and it seemed that I was only a few stations from where I needed to be. How extraordinary! When we are lost, there is a heightened feeling of alertness that guides us through the most desperate of circumstances. We must surrender to this primitive instinct, since it has our best interest at heart. The stations passed quickly, and my stop appeared. I felt more satisfaction than I felt relief. Being able to trust my instincts gave me a greater appreciation for my internal system. I felt stronger and more capable. The sunlight shattered the relative darkness of the tunnels, as I came into the open streets of Paris. It was an awakening, with the old buildings resting securely on the land amid the commotion of conflicting traffic and rushing pedestrians. It took me some moments to get my bearings. Tables and chairs were comfortably laid out on the sidewalks to offer solace to the wayward traveler. I took the silent offer and crossed the street to a series of chairs and tables that had the right look and which faced Notre Dome. With a glass of red wine and some cheese, I reviewed my victory over uncertainty and lostness.

To strike out in a new direction is always difficult. It is an uprooting that can cause mental and physical pain, and, sometimes, we wonder whether it is worth the struggle of it. There is within us a yearning, a feeling that it is time to do or see something else. When this comes to us, and we ignore it, our restlessness gets chambered up until it becomes rage and festers in hidden corners of our bodies, causing discomfort and eventually disease. We are creatures that seek to grow and change throughout our lives. When we hold back because we are lost or afraid, we rob ourselves of realizing our greatest strengths. It is our adventure to seek out new paths, new routes to discover who we are and what our passions are. It may seem like a simple excursion, but within its scope is a wonderland of personal doubts, dreams, and myths. This adventure is like Alice's when she fell through the opening. *How can I deal with the mysteries of life, with its strange adventures of tangled feelings, failures, and confrontations?* we wonder. As I sipped my wine, I thought how wonderful it was to be in a strange place, seeing with refreshed eyes the sights and sounds that were newly about me. Life was suddenly fresher, more vital, and more immediate. It was a confusing trip. The uncertainty of it all brought out a new wonder and beauty to things. Our rut in life is that we don't really see what is in front of us. We become too trapped by our certainty, our familiarity. It takes being thrown off-course, or momentarily losing direction, to bring us to a stronger and brighter vision of things. It might be the loss of a job, going through a divorce, sudden sickness, a passing infatuation, or a vision of loveliness on another ferry.

I remember reading a passage by Somerset Maugham in which he described seeing a woman whose loveliness stayed with him throughout his life. He was on one ferry, and she was on another ferry going in the opposite direction. He realized, in that instant, that he would miss her, that there would always be a longing to meet her. It can be just an instant's experience that changes how you see things and what you look forward to. Creativity is about exploring these moments and using them to develop who you are and what can give you a sense of beauty and inspiration. This will energize your spirit, so that each of your days gives you pleasure and a sense of satisfaction.

I realize, in looking back over my past and, in particular, my experiences getting lost in Dallas and Paris, that I have gained so much from my decisions to explore the unknown and daring routes of life. Mechanical repetitions of daily activities lead to depression and a lack of trust in self. You gain yourself by losing yourself when you explore new territories, whether within yourself or outside in the world. The struggle of finding out who you are involves accepting the uncertainties of life and recognizing when you are lost. So often people's discontent comes from their lack of knowing themselves and what they truly want—or neglecting what inspires them, because it seems too impractical and out of their reach.

There are no easy ways of finding what you want in this life and creating a pathway toward it. Your life expression can only come as a result of your search to find it—to find meaning for your life that meets your fondest expectations. You can wait until the end of your days to suddenly, regretfully, consider what you have *not* done with your life. But why wait? Why not discover what resides within your creative soul as well as the extent of your being? I had a friend ask me the other day, "Why study creativity?" It was a question that no one had ever asked me before, so I had to think. Why is it so important for anyone to develop and expand their creativity? And a single word entered my mind: beauty. We should learn about creativity so that we can develop a sense of beauty, so that we can recognize it in all the places it exists. Our ability to see beauty allows us to transcend the mundane and the transitory.

To really look at a sculpture by Rodin is to confront the yearnings and tragedies of life. It is to see and feel the texture of life so graphically and meaningfully expressed that you cannot deny the wonder and brilliance of it. But, at the same time, we are exposed to the fleeting romance that it portrays, the passions that have waned in the mix of arms and legs that is permanently confined to a concrete expression for our love and enrichment. We have felt the touch of humanity against our eyes and against our souls—to reward us with the sight of life. Appreciation may come spontaneously to some of us, but for most it is a learned ability. To perceive beauty is to bring our lives to a level where the simplest of expressions can bring us to ecstatic heights. When we explore our own creativity, we move closer to all expressions of beauty. As we understand our own creativeness, we become a part of the universal flow of energy and creativity.

To lie in a hammock as it gently rocks, and to perceive the solitary flight of a long-beaked bird, as you follow its flow and glide above the heated land, is to touch the essence of beauty. The perceived bird brings together the harmonious parts of the scene to instill peace and a sense of continuous motion to the painter, the writer, and the visual artist for their work. To join with them in the creative expression is to bring your life into alignment with the beauty of mankind. Beauty that takes us into ourselves and out of ourselves so that we can participate in the great myths and stories of our humanity is what allows us to reach our potential as individuals. It is the tension of art, the tension of lostness and confusion that drives us to an understanding of our individual potential and worth. Beauty enriches our lives and gives expression to our pain. To not seek it out is to lose an important aspect of the life experience.

As in Rodin's *The Eternal Idol,* there is the strain between heaven and hell which shows us in an image, in a sculpture, the forces that gave birth to us, that lifted our spirits, and that might destroy us: unrequited love. Rainer Maria Rilke's comment about this sculpture is: "There is something of the mood of purgatory alive within this work. Heaven is near, but has not yet been attained; hell is close, but has not yet been forgotten." But in filling ourselves with the beauty of the sculpture, we have begun to understand the power of the mind that is within each of us. We overcome the rudeness of our existence by comprehending beauty—even the poignant beauty of an almost-surrender. We reach fulfillment of our potential by developing our innate creativeness through exploration and risk-taking.

A simple cup of coffee in a yellow cup on a blue tablecloth can make you feel that all of life is wonderful, as you can take the next breath and feel the pleasure of a new morning. The ultimate meaning of our lives comes from the montage of our stories that we have slowly pieced together. To view them requires our creative expression, our wonder, and our passion. The joy of the routes is in the experience. The adventure is always before us.

Flower in the window

Striking the Match

Take a new road and see where it leads. Allow yourself the experience of not knowing where you are going to end up, and see what you find. There may be a new something that is just waiting for you to discover it, as you wind through unfamiliar roads. Make your Sunday drive an adventure. You never know what you might find when you do not know where you are going.

Write about an incident that confused you and tell how you handled that confusion. What did you learn? How did you overcome it? Our quest for knowledge comes out of situations when we don't know.

Take a trip to the library and spend fifteen minutes wandering through the shelves with the idea that you are there to find some book that will be meaningful to you. Seek without prejudgment. Look at books lying on tables or slightly hanging out from shelves, and select ones that somehow attract you. Quickly review each one you come across, and only select the one that moves you the most. Then read it—to discover something new and beneficial to you.

A WILDERNESS
Chapter Seven

When I was five or six years old, we lived in a three-room railroad apartment, in the Bronx, on the third floor. At night, I would lie in my bed and watch the ceiling with its moving shadows caused by the passing cars' headlights. It turned into a kind of game for me. If the shadows went from left to right, I would ask myself which way the car was going and vice versa. I am not sure I ever came up with a conclusion to the puzzle, but it kept me entertained during those nights before sleep. The worst part of the night, however, was when a shadow went past a closet door and made it appear as if it were opening up. My attention would become so focused on the closet and its movement that my heart began to beat faster, and I felt very anxious. I would stare at the closet and hold my breath as the next light flashed across the slightly "opened" closet. It caused me to lie very still and watch for the slightest movement that could then send me into a panic.

Although this childish imagination of closet and under-the-bed danger has left me, there is the inheritance of fear that has lingered through the years and affected my life's unfolding. So often fear has entered my thoughts and controlled my actions. As I got older, I was afraid that I was not smart. I was afraid that I had no talent. I was afraid to speak in front of small groups of people. I was afraid of the water. This kind of thinking can lead us into hesitation, doubt, and inaction.

As we move into opening our creative natures, we will discover that fear and doubt are with us like the shadows on the childhood wall. They sneak into our consciousness and give us the sense that we are not skilled enough, or strong enough, or intelligent enough to do the things we say we can do. Doubt can distort our purpose and lead us to surrender before we have even fully started. Sometimes the uncertainty of an outcome gives us hesitation. Will we succeed? Will we get the grade? Will we be promoted? These questions drive us to the edge of ourselves and cause us to pause and perhaps give in to the feelings of weakness that have taken hold. Although a part of us is trying to protect us from the uncertainties of new experiences, we need to push past the fear and the doubt and overcome the weakness of the moment. It is so sad sometimes to see people give up on their dreams or goals when we know that they can do it. They just need to persist, to try one more day, to watch the shadows on the wall with amusement instead of fear.

In moving from white belt to yellow belt in Tae Kwon Do, I had to perform the basic moves that I had learned during the white belt stages of development. We were in a large room above a bowling alley. The wood floor was highly polished, and one long wall was completely covered with full-length mirrors. On the day of the test, the temperature was very high. Two windows were opened to let in some air, as a large rotating fan buzzed back and forth, giving little relief to the people in the crowded room. Guests of students, as well as students from different classes, were all anxiously surrounding the practice and test area. Tension hung like the punching bags that dangled from the ceiling on heavy chains. Our doubts would slip in between the firing of our synapses. We felt initially strong and confident that all would go well—until a shadow would cross our minds, and a closet slightly open, and we would be confronted with a familiar fear. I carefully watched the students who were called on first, as they went through the routine (the form), so that I could reinforce the moves in my mind. However, as I waited, I became more and more aware of my discomfort and hesitations. I wondered if I was really ready.

Perhaps it would be better to wait. Even if I had practiced it so many times, I felt I just might not be ready for the test, the interview, the branching out into a new direction. As I waited, I could feel the sweat within my gi (my uniform) moving down my back without my control. I did not want to feel anxious. And the more I tried not to be nervous, the more nervous I became. My name was called, and my ears went red. I quickly moved to the middle of the test area and bowed. I assumed the first stance, and then continued on through the movements until I reached a point where I could not remember the next move. I did not know which way to turn. I immediately went into confusion and basically froze. My sensei (teacher) asked me to continue. I said that I did not know my next move. He told me to sit down and watch, and he would call on me again.

There are times in life when darkness overtakes us, and our movements and thinking become sluggish and forgetful. We hang in the uncertainty of life's unfolding, hesitant and unable to see the next steps we need to take. Although we would prefer not to go through this wilderness of fear and darkness, it is the only way in which we can truly find ourselves and our creativeness. As Joseph Conrad suggested in *The Heart of Darkness*, there is a primitive part of us that resides in this lost world of our subconscious and influences our judgment and actions. We need to confront the darkness and fears within us—so that we can move beyond them and paint our fearful animals upon the cave walls of our minds in the primal ritual of protection and containment. Let them join the mythology of our spirit so that they can be identified and overcome. We succeed by confronting. We succeed by going through the fearful steps of our doubt and darkness.

As I sat cross-legged, attentive to movements of the form, I realized the direction I needed to go to get past the place where I had gotten stuck. It was so easy, and yet I had messed up. Sitting there aggravated me and made me angry with myself. How could I blow it like that? What was wrong with me? In the midst of talking to myself, I was called to do the test over. Mumbling in my mind, I began the movements again, going through them as precisely as I could, until I reached the same place I had gotten stuck before—and stopped. In spite of all my watching and thinking about what I should do, it had happened again. I stood frozen in this position with no sense of what direction I needed to go in. Again the sensei asked me to continue. I could not. I had to sit back down and watch again. It is frustrating when we get stuck and can't seem to get out of it. The more we complain to ourselves about how it should not be like this—*You should know better! How can you be so stupid?*—the more we stay stuck and continue to do the same things over and over again. Focus, concentration, and discipline are the only skills that will help you out of this failure to move. As soon as I focused on calming myself and concentrated on the movements that came after the stuck point, I began to feel my confidence returning. In controlling my conversation to myself, I was able to reach a place of more control within myself. The third time I was asked to do the test, I made it through without hesitation and completed the form correctly. It was a wonderful feeling to have finally succeeded. If I had given up after the first two attempts, I would have missed the joy of the accomplishment. In addition, I had learned that proper preparation included controlling my thoughts as well as my body. If my sensei had not given me the opportunity to redo my martial art forms, I could have remained stuck and fearful. It is all about confronting and pushing past the doubts and hesitation that come up for us.

Many people try to hide from their fears and blocks. By pulling back from the edge, they attempt to create a new scenario, so that they do not have to deal with the problem areas of their life. However, by avoiding their blocks, they only leave themselves open to going through it all over again and dealing with the same blocks (except perhaps with new people and environments). A benefit of creative expression is its ability to move you beyond habitual repetitions. You don't need to go through yet another relationship, another mistake in judgment, or another business failure. The repetition can end when you simply accept the challenge of addressing your own fears, your own wilderness.

The way in which we go through some of our fears may be elusive to us. We may be convinced that we are trying our very best to get through them, or over them—but we are hiding within our minds our actual evasive actions. Most of us are aware of situations where we have been basically blind to what was really going on. How often have we been told by our friends, after we broke up with someone, that they knew this person was really bad for us and it wasn't going to last? In some cases, we may have even been married to the person without recognizing the irreconcilable differences that were part of the relationship. Our minds regularly create the reality that we believe is there but really isn't. It is one of the reasons, as Henry Ford said, "Whether you think you can, or you think you can't, you are right." Our willingness to regularly review our lives, and our beliefs about ourselves and the world around us, is an important aspect of our growth and our ability to achieve the outcomes that we most want. We need a good mentor, sensei, or friend, who can help us review our weaknesses as well as the fears which prevent us from achieving our goals. We cannot do it alone. We need the vision and support of others to foster our own personal vision for our lives.

In a culture that idolizes the Lone Ranger, it is sometimes difficult for us to ask for help—but it is necessary. Our ability to see ourselves is limited and fraught with distortion. With the help of a good mentor, we can receive the support we need to go through the movements again and go through the "mind limits" again, so that we can see what is about us clearly and can make the right moves.

In a workshop that was designed to help people recognize their strategies for confronting fear and risk, there was an exercise that dealt with breaking an arrow with the soft part of the neck. It was necessary to have the metal tip of the arrow strategically placed just above your chest in that little soft spot of your neck, while someone else held the arrow. Everyone was told that as long as they followed instructions everything would go fine, and they would succeed in breaking the arrow. However, each of the participants was asked to sign a waiver to ensure that they understood they would proceed at their own risk and the workshop would not be liable for any mishaps. The signing of the document actually increased the tension that people felt for the exercise. After the exercise had been described and demonstrated a couple of times, the individual groups had to decide who within the group would be the first participants.

Since the exercise needed two people, one holding the arrow and the other walking into the arrow, it took a while for everyone to determine who was going first and which group of two they wanted to be in. Although there was some tension, everything went smoothly in the groups, until it was a woman called Anita's turn. She had watched almost everyone else go, and there were just two groups left, hers and one other. She saw their enthusiasm and joy when the arrow was successfully broken. She knew it could be done. Her partner had completed it with no trouble. However, Anita had a lot of hesitation. When the arrow was placed against her neck, she pulled back. She said she was not ready. The arrow was again placed against her and, seeing her hesitation, everyone began to encourage her to just move forward. She took a step but pulled her head and neck so far back that there was no real forward movement. The others continued to encourage her to move forward. Every time she moved forward with her feet, her body kept moving as far backward as it could without falling over. It was an extraordinary sight to see, because it was clear that Anita thought that she was moving forward, while, in truth, she was bending backward as far as she was stepping forward. She did not realize what she was doing any more than we realize what we are doing when we are in our own situations of fear or uncertainty. We feel as if we are committed to moving forward. We think we have mustered the courage to move forward. But we do not get to the next step.

Unwilling to admit our fear, our *stuckness*, we seek escape. Anita wanted to wait. She wanted to wait until the next couple went. And they did go, and then it was back to Anita. She said she had decided she did not want to do it. We all told her how easy it really was and that she needed to do it. Finally she acquiesced and had the arrow nestled in the softness of her neck just above her rib cage. She said that the point was sharp and was hurting her neck. She said that this arrow might be stronger than the others that broke. She said that she was moving forward, and it just wasn't breaking. She said that she didn't think it was a good exercise. She said that she was *trying*.

Finally, she stepped forward without bending backward, and the arrow tensed between Anita's neck and the hands of the holder. It suddenly arched up toward the ceiling and snapped. In an instant, Anita broke through her fear and felt an explosive sense of joy. She was hugged by each member of the group and congratulated for her triumph. Anita, with tears in her eyes, thanked everyone for helping her through it and not letting her give up. Alone we can falter and deny that we are faltering. It is easy to come up with reasons why something is not going to work or to say we have been trying our best but it just isn't happening. Part of developing our creativity is to discover new ways to overcome our blocks and hesitations. It is also wise to seek out mentors and workshops, which will expand our repertoires of strategies for realizing our loves and passions in life. We are easily deceived by our minds into thinking that we know what is taking place, but, like Anita, we do not realize how we are sabotaging our own efforts. We must persist, if we are to achieve the joy and satisfaction that we are so close to, by overcoming our fears of the unknown.

There are many parts to our wilderness. From childhood it grows, becoming wilder and more complicated as the years go by. Our parents, our teachers, our friends, our enemies, and our lovers all contribute to the maze that becomes our private wilderness. Each of us must enter it, so that we can move beyond our fears and doubts and move beyond the shadow animals that inhabit our beautiful wilderness. Often we are afraid to enter, holding on to old comforts, unwilling to experience the more primitive and earthy side of ourselves. It is the untamed and wild that live in this hidden place of tangled vegetation and ferocious beasts. But we are all drawn to the wild side of things and are curious about its nature. It is this very nature that inspires, that brings us to expressing our passions, that drives us to discover, to paint, to write, and to explore the unknown. It is why Paul Gauguin went to Tahiti, why Chris Angel pushes his magic to the limits; why Dostoevsky wrote *Crime and Punishment.* We spin in a world of our own making. We arrange the materials and experiences of it into patterns that currently make sense to us.

Below the surface, however, are the ruling forces that guide or shove us into directions that can be either alarming or expected. There exists the tension between our conscious selves and our wilderness. However we may struggle against the forces of the wilderness, they are there to cajole, entice, and aggravate. It is these forces that can enrich our lives and give us an understanding of ourselves that will help us through the nights and lonely parts of our lives. To truly grasp what *you* are about is one of the great joys of life. To enter into the wilderness of *you,* so that you can confront the energy and drive that is at your center—that is your soul, the passion that will sustain you throughout your life. It is why the journey within is so important. Expression of your creativeness upholds you and gives meaning to your days.

There is restlessness, a roaming feeling that extends out of this land of dreams, secrets, and powerful urges. It has us reaching for some kind of accomplishment, of which we are uncertain. Our lives spill out from its mountain streams, high lakes, and daring hills—from its tall trees and secret caves—rushing us forward to seek some stability to allay isolated volcanic eruptions. Our wilderness keeps us tense and uncomfortable when we have not embraced it, when we think of it as dark and threatening. Since we are not one thing, we must all traverse the interior landscape, so that we can find the source of our rivers and discover the areas of light that reside between the tall trees and sparkling streams of our subconscious. In this rich territory, each of us can unearth our loves, our passions, and our abiding yearnings, so that we can express them in the story of our deepest selves. Unlocking the door to our wilderness may present some initial discomfort, but the verdant land within is the jewel of our lives.

Some years ago, at a NLP seminar that I was taking, the facilitator, Jan Marzelek, put a cloth over my head and asked what I saw under the safety of the cloth. For some reason, I saw the image of a Harlequin with a ruffled white collar and a decorative black-and-white body suit. He was smiling and very whimsical and charming. Jan asked, "Why is he smiling?"

"Because my father is dead," I said, with a certainty of truth that leaped forth from my wilderness. Its expression caused a dramatic change in me. I felt the power of the loss and immediately revisited the scene of my father's death and funeral. My father died in my arms, when I was twelve, on a Sunday morning, in brilliant sunlight. The shock and the quickness of it froze my mind and left me numb and distant for some time after his death, perhaps even until that day. As much as we believe we are aware of the things about us, in times of tragedy our brain shuts out whatever we cannot grasp or do not want to see. I did not cry. I could not cry. I went through the experience as if I were a stranger to the person who was crowded with flowers, looking very pale but rosy cheeked. He seemed like a mannequin lying peacefully within a solitary container. Puffy white fabric reached about his figure, suggesting innocence in the finality of death.

As I sat under the cloth, the terror of the day came back with a power that had not been present before. I began to cry for all the days I had not cried. I spilled out the story from the hidden lake of regrets. My mind burned as the words rushed more and more quickly from its secret places, expressing my separation from his death. I could see myself running faster and faster away from the feelings within that were so wild and disturbing. Within the echoing sadness of the funeral, I could only smile and greet people as if things were okay, as if the world had not suddenly come to an end, as if it were all a dream that would soon end and things would go back to normal.

My mother said to me that I had to cry, since everyone at the funeral was talking about my lack of sadness. I had to fake-cry to still the family and friends, to express what I could not express; I had to fake when there was no strength to feel. I had loved my father dearly. He stood above everyone else. His quiet way had filtered into my soul, and I screamed for him not to end. Under the covering of the cloth, I roamed through the rooms of sadness and loss. I raged at the darkness that had for so long hovered within. My father was finally dead, and I cried for my weakness; I cried for my faking; I cried for my dad. And I cried for me.

When the cover was lifted, most of the people who were part of the seminar had left the room, since they had been so affected by the unfolding of my story. It was a day of release, when old fears and regrets were mourned and brought into perspective. A sense of relief swiftly passed through my veins, giving my body a new peace. I was extremely grateful for the insight that I was given as a result of Jan's willingness to facilitate expression. As we approach the deepest parts of ourselves, we have the opportunity to alleviate the regrets, failures, and losses that we have experienced. It does not matter how old or young we are—there are things that happen to us that must be expressed if we are to live our lives with fullness and joy. Unresolved emotions that are contained within the caves and crevices of our minds are sources of illness for us. Unexpressed, they fester and spread through our whole system to infect and disturb our peace and joy. The importance of our individual expression cannot be overemphasized.

How often have we wondered why we give ourselves over to weaknesses and relationships that undermine who we are—thereby accepting a lesser image of ourselves? The difficulty of confrontation is that it is uncomfortable and sometimes painful. The abiding proposition, however, is to bring yourself to a place of strength, creativeness, and joy. These qualities are within our reach each day. We must focus on our lives as if our lives depended upon it. As much as we might want to avoid discipline, we must avoid the regularity of doing things—it is the one way to overcome what oftentimes holds us back. No matter what we want to do in our lives, creative expression will give us a path that will release the richest part of ourselves. Do we give in to the urge to act, the urge to write, the urge to play music? What we have is all the experiences that we have gone through since we entered this world. We can wish we had been born into a better world, but it will not help us use the world we have. Each day gives us an opportunity to see into the wilderness that we have constructed. Each day gives us the chance to draw on our caves walls magnificent images of our roaming beasts. Each day gives us the prospect of discovering the light in the forest, so that we can enjoy ourselves for the wonder that we are. There is great beauty in our wilderness. We only need to risk finding it.

City visions

Striking the Match

Seek out a mentor. Find someone you can talk to who will give you open and frank information about yourself, so that you can see yourself more clearly. It could be a good friend, a life coach, a therapist, or a workshop leader. The experience could be invaluable to you. Take the chance, and explore.

Find a workshop or seminar that is designed to help improve your communication skills, your personal development, your art, or your health. We all need support and community to help us in our struggles with our forest. Accept the challenge, and seek out environments that will help you grow.

Write about your forest. Write about the things that have bothered you through the years and that you have held back in expressing. Use this opportunity to express this deepest part of yourself. Paint on your cave wall the animals of your fears.

The Blacksmith
Chapter Eight

Sweat ran down the arms of the blacksmith, as he stoked the fire and prepared the next piece of ore to be fired up. The man's arms were thick with muscle, and his body moved with strength and certainty. Years of training and experience had been weaved into his sinews, so that the slightest task was performed with skill and intuitive accuracy. The blacksmith symbolizes man's rise out of the darkness of isolated tribes with limited vision into the light of imagination and active communities.

The richness of the blacksmith's fire formed its own dreams and fantasies that leapt into the stirrings of the human heart and mind, producing new visions of the future. Civilization came from the heat of its pit, reared up through tools of agriculture and war; even the wheel was precisely ribboned with metal by the falling hammers of the smithy. It was the blacksmith who kept the towns supplied with needed ornaments and tools. He was the one who, through fire and water, molded the passing generations. He understood the secrets of ores and the combining of metals to produce materials that were stronger and more durable. The iron ore was hammered and rehammered, as it was folded over and over again, until the impurities had been driven from its mass by the sweatful workings of his hand. It was the art of the blacksmith that molded communities and brought life to a new level of sophistication.

We all are blacksmiths in our own lives. How well we use the hammer and the anvil will determine how well we grow as individuals. We are a rich source of materials, of ore that requires refinement and molding. We must not miss the opportunity to use them, so that we can overcome what might be holding us back. By using the ore that we have gathered over the years through our many experiences, we can develop new strengths and insights. The recognition of who we are and what we are is essential in helping us move away from fear and limitations. It is important to know that to overcome our deepest hesitations and weaknesses; we need to put them in the fire, so that we can recast them. Although we may feel uncomfortable about doing this, there is usually no other way to conquer them. Unless we are in the fire, we may hang on to our old behaviors well beyond their usefulness.

In graduate school, I was required to give an hour-long presentation of a research project that I had done. I was required to do this presentation in order to pass the class. I had gotten through almost all my previous classes without the embarrassment of talking in front of the class. This was the only class that finally exposed me to a serious speaking engagement and trauma. I was so shy during this period of my life that I always planned when I would answer a question in class, so I would not be at risk of having to talk too long. I would respond only to a question that required the least number of words to answer. In addition, I always sat in the front, knowing that it was a position that usually received the least number of questions directed to it. I had been safe for so many years—until this final class.

When the day came, I was in a panic. I could feel my face flush, and I was not even there yet. For some reason, days like these seemed to drag on as if I were behind a truck in a never-ending journey, like a bad dream that is not a dream. Finally, the class began, and I anxiously waited as other students gave their presentations. I opted to go last. What a mistake! Every minute was like an hour to me. Even with the air-conditioning blasting, I was a furnace.

When it was my turn, I quickly got up and turned to face the class.

Redness flowed through every pore of my body as my mouth went dry and my mind went blank. With my paper firmly gripped in both hands, I began reading. My voice droned and warbled through a maze of incomprehensible words. The paper and my hands shook so much that it was difficult for me to read. Between staring at the paper and reading, I was able to collect some spit to swallow. It did not help much, but I had reached the part in my presentation when I could turn off the lights and begin the slide show that I had prepared. Although my throat was dry, and I was still in the throes of anxiety, I was able to hide in the darkness and read without being totally seen. When it was over, I was exhausted. And I passed the class.

How could I remold myself? How could I overcome the fear that took over when I was in front of a group of people? To deal with this challenge, I—either through a case of sheer brilliance or stupidity—placed myself in front of a group of teenagers to teach high school English. Talk about fire. It was a truly frightening experience, especially since I had such a strong fear of people. There were days when the fire was so intense that I thought I would just give up and never think about teaching again. I began to pray for the end of the semester, or for it to be quickly swallowed by a hungry behemoth so it could be instantly digested. But the end took longer in coming than I had wanted, and the beast never showed up. It may have had something to do with the pay.

However, with the passing of days and classes, I became more and more able to speak with confidence and enthusiasm. When you are uptight or tense, your body and mind are not at their best. They tighten up and give off a restrictive and unfriendly attitude. I learned that when you fear, you need to move into your fear, or it will hold you back and prevent you from exploring other avenues of joy and self-expression.

Although it took time, I now love speaking in front of people. I love sharing my knowledge with as many people as I can. If I had not taken the chance to enter the fire, I would never have discovered this wonderful world of speaking and meeting people. Since I had had a very confined childhood mixed with sickness and lack of friends, it could have permanently kept me from any meaningful interactions or kept me from addressing my fears and hesitations. But my willingness to learn and explore gave me the courage to enter the fires of life and pick up the hammer that was my birthright. With the hammer firmly in hand, I find my life continually remolds itself on the anvil of experience.

You cannot shy away from the fire, the hammer, or the anvil. They are an essential part of your life experience. If you attempt to stand back from the furnace, you will perhaps miss life's greatest gifts: realization of self and the joy of expressing the quintessential part of who you are. We all long to do something with our lives that is meaningful to us, and this originates in the deepest part of ourselves. Some call it *your legend*, and others call it *your bliss*, but whatever you call it, you will always be restless until you have confronted and expressed this part of yourself.

In order to mold the ingot, you must initiate. As the tree pushes up against gravity, so must you. It requires practice and failing. It requires practice and succeeding. It requires that you decide what you want. Lack of decision causes hesitation, which causes delay, which causes a decade to pass without you even realizing that it has gone. Appreciation of a tree can come from your trial drawings of it or your photographs. A tree offers a wonderful study of the present moment. Its leaves have different shapes and veins and colors. How beautiful it is in sunlight, with brilliant light greens and dark greens, with streaks of brown and dusty whites. You become caught in the magic of it, the intensity and the immediacy of it. I have always been amazed at the watercolors of Andrew Wyeth. You can almost feel the woodenness, the roughness of the painted foliage. I would touch the page upon which the image was printed just to see if I would experience the sensations that seemed so close to my fingertips. But the page was smooth. However, I was there, totally into the moment of my reaching hand—as you can be there the moment you truly see a leaf, or a painting, or a decision that you need to make; you can hold back the passing of time just long enough to fully appreciate it. Making a decision is the first step toward molding or remolding your ingot. It is also the conscious awareness of being immediately involved in a current moment of time. Art requires that you are present.

Openness to the moment gives you possibilities that are not available to you when you are closed and locked down in your thinking as to what you can or cannot do. The first time I drew I was sitting in front of the television watching Edward Albee being interviewed. It was interesting, but I was a little restless. As I was watching close-ups of his face, I wondered what it would be like to draw it. I have no idea where that thought came from. But I picked up a pad and started to draw his face from the TV screen. I totally lost what was being said, as I concentrated on his face and the upper part of his body. It had never occurred to me how interesting it could be to try to get a face on paper by using lines that curved and straightened out. I began rushing a bit, as I realized that the show would soon end. I still have this crude drawing that was so casually drawn so many years ago. But it was the first fall of the hammer.

I had a student recently who had been asked to keep a journal as part of the workshop. Initially, she had no particular desire to write in a journal, since she felt it was an intrusion into her busy personal life. She was working full-time and had two children and a husband. She said that she did not really have the time to sit down and write her random thoughts. However, as the workshop progressed, she took a dip into writing one weekend afternoon and found herself, as I had done with the drawing of Albee, totally immersed in the process of putting her thoughts on paper. The train of her thoughts intrigued her, and she became more and more curious about what would come up. The process had its own heady way of bringing her further and further into its realm. By the end of the workshop, she had filled one composition book with thoughts and activities and was looking forward to starting another one. The hammer was falling again.

The path to our creative self is mixed. It is not present only when we are engaged in writing, drawing, or pottery making. We see it within tasks that help us reach deep into ourselves and show courage, determination, and a realization of overcoming what is holding us back. Throughout the ages, we have been instructed to seek within for the answers to our lives. Confronting the fire is about confronting fears, and in that confrontation you will unleash your internal power and creativeness. To overcome any obstacle, you need your creativeness to see alternative ways for accomplishing the task—the remolding. We are sometimes blind to our own abilities to be creative. If you have gotten through the many difficulties that life has presented to you, you have used this unique power over and over again. It is always with you. However, without conscious use it can become dormant, and you may miss the fact that you have it. When we are discouraged and lose hope, we can ignore the very part of ourselves that can bring us out of that darkness.

Standing at the edge of the fire brings us into the reality of our present moment. If we are dissatisfied, we can take steps to change that dissatisfaction—through action. If we feel afraid, we can take hold of the fear and change it for a new feeling of confidence—by overcoming fear. If we are lost, we can find our way through inner revelations and intuitions that reside within the byways of our synaptic jumps.

When I was about six, I was at Castle Hill pool with my mom. It was a wonderfully sunny day, and I was running around with some of my friends and playing shoot-'em-up games. With our tiny fingers as guns, we were wild cowboys taming the West. As we ran around the pool, the father of one of my friends caught his son and flipped him into the pool. He went under the water for a few seconds, and then he was up on top again, swimming quickly to the pool's edge, since he was in the deep end. He was laughing and yelling at his father. His father grabbed his hand and pulled him out. As soon as he was out, he said, "Do it again, Daddy." He was again flipped out into the glistening pool. I stood on the side in amazement. Suddenly, Eddy's father grabbed me, and I went flying into the water. I hit the water frozen with fright.

As a result, I can still see the light; it was diffused by the surface of the water, as I sank to the bottom of the pool. Although fear drifted away from me, I had no idea what to do. There were men coming down toward me. But I was a still being, transfixed by the volume of water. I was grabbed by one of men and pulled to the surface, where I think I must have been lifted out of the water. I started coughing and saw a lot of people around me. The man who had thrown me in kept saying over and over, "I am so sorry. I am so sorry; I didn't think he would just ..." Water coughed out of my mouth; I suddenly felt cold. Sounds blended together, including my mother's voice, as I regained myself. Finally, I stood up, with shaky legs. I only wanted to leave the area. I wanted to disappear, to escape the concerned crowd and the feelings that were rushing through me.

Not too long afterward, although I am not certain exactly how long, I was in Staten Island at the beach, with a friend of mine, Marty. We had been playing in the water for a while. I was beginning to feel more confident with jumping the waves and falling into the water. I steadily ventured a little further out, until I was probably too far out. Without warning, or as a result of me not paying attention, a wave knocked me down and under. My eyes went instantly closed. I had a distinct understanding that I was under the water, and it was not a good thing. But Technicolor dreams with Mickey Mouse and Pluto were immediately taking over my imagination. I was so absorbed by the color and the playful story that was quickly unfolding that I did not consider anything else. But from someplace deep within my spirit a mantra began. Get up. Get up. Get up. It was so difficult to pull myself from the dream, from the colors. When I finally stood up, there was no one close to me and no one looking for me. I began to cough and cough and droplets of water shot out of my mouth. I quickly left the water and ran to my mother. Everyone was surprised when I told them of my water dream. Then there was deep concern.

Many years have passed since these two incidents occurred, and they are more part of memory than they are consciousness. The things that limit us, however, never really leave us; we just are not aware of them. They lurk below the surface to expose themselves in subtle and sometimes unrecognizable ways. It might be fear of making a commitment that causes us to pull back from a good relationship, or, in this case, fear of water. I was in Nassau with a close friend who wanted to go snorkeling. Even though I had not been in the water for a good number of years, I did not want to hang back and prevent her from having a partner in this adventure. So I agreed, with just the slightest trepidation. In my mind, I saw a lovely beach with a flat ocean and the ability to touch shore, if needed. The reality was that there was more depth to the water than I expected, rolling waves, and solid land only off in the distance.

My mind spun, as the boat rocked and we prepared to go in. The life jacket that was wrapped around my chest did not indicate safety to me; it only gave me a further unsettled feeling within. However, securely fitted and with fins in my hands, I descended into the deep water. Grasping the ladder with one hand, I tried to secure one of the fins to my foot with the other hand. With determination and an unwillingness to cower in front of my girlfriend, I managed to secure the fins, and we were on our way, or, I should say, I was on my way. My girlfriend was already seeking out the wonderful coral and playful fish that inhabited the world hidden beneath the water. As I heard my breathing coming in and out of my mouthpiece, I realized how unfamiliar this setting was to me. I did know that I had been born out of this watery environment at one time, but its current strangeness seeped deeper into my thoughts the longer I swam away from the boat.

It was such an odd feeling to be hanging ten feet or so above fish and sand. My mind tried to understand how it was possible. All sizes of fish went by, with indifference and mission. It was eerie and beautiful. My girlfriend came close and took my hand; she began to lead me toward something she had found that she wanted me to see. Suddenly, I had a sense of being too far from the boat. I broke away from her hand and began turning toward the boat. My breathing became a little more labored, and some water entered the tube, which caused a gurgling sound. I thought it was filling. I brought my head out of the water just in time to get smacked by a wave. I could see the boat about twenty-five feet away, but the waves were higher than I expected, and they kept me bobbing up and down. I put my head back down into the water, only to hear my breathing laboring unevenly. The water was now dark, and the waves were washing over me. I could feel myself losing it.

My childhood experience of sinking to the bottom suddenly overtook me. I struggled with trying to remain calm, but a whole series of memories rushed in, causing increased distrust and fear. Lights from an operating room and the smell of ether intruded, as I felt the waves and water, heavy and uncontrollable, all packed against my mind—until I began to struggle in the water, feeling lost and about to succumb to its swelling willfulness.

As I tried to swim to the boat, the waves seemed to keep me at an equal distance from it. Finally, with my hands waving, and a desperate call for help as I bobbed and swallowed, I was thrown a round life preserver. It floated in the water before me as a dirty white aspiration that I might not make. I kicked and struggled with ever-increasing loudness and abandon. There was no thought in my head that the life jacket I had on would really prevent me from drowning. My fear locked out everything except getting to the white circle and saving myself. When we fear, we are trapped in our limited vision. We prevent ourselves from using our own resources as well as additional options that might be available.

Once I grabbed the life preserver, however, I was quickly pulled to the boat. After struggling up the ladder and being seated, I realized what a profound hole I had dug for myself. I would now be looked upon as a leper to the water world, to be shunned by those who had been blessed by Poseidon. I had lost face with my girlfriend and the captain. I felt truly dejected and uncomfortable. However, I learned a valuable lesson. What you do not confront will remain within you, and it will weaken you.

All of us have something that prevents us from realizing what we most want. It might be fear of water, success, commitment, failure, or speaking in public—but, whatever it is, there is a way to overcome its impinging intrusion. Standing in front of the furnace and allowing ourselves to feel the flame is the only way we can achieve a remolding of ourselves. What holds us back many times is that we believe it will be painful and difficult to do. On the contrary, once the decision is made, the remolding can be enjoyable as well as rewarding. It is the creative process that opens up new ways for us to overcome the struggles we have within. If we prevent this creative life flow from taking place, we remain confined to our fears and our cold iron-held positions. We may believe we are right, but this only prevents us from moving to new places in our lives. To accept the fire is to understand the importance of confronting our fears.

As a way of confronting my fear of water, I began reading about sailing, the beauty of the sea, and the adventures that people have had while exploring the waters of the Caribbean. I began regularly visiting beaches to walk along at the water's edge, to feel its coolness, and to jump into its blue and whiteness to experience its support and vitality. I began to learn about things that were attractive to me about the ocean and about being out in the water. I realized that I was fighting it and not allowing the natural process to take control. I started going into a pool regularly to feel the pleasure of this enveloping liquid. When I tensed, I began to concentrate on relaxing. I did not berate myself when I became anxious or uncomfortable. With each step, I slowly gained more confidence. I approached the fire with the creativeness that was within my spirit, so that I could transform the fear that held me back. I began watching people swim and noticed how they moved their bodies differently than I did. I mimicked their movements, in my mind first, then when I was in the water. The power is within us to transform our lives at any stage. As my images of water became less foreboding, and my language reinforced this new perspective, I became more interested in it. I became more comfortable with it. With the accumulating experiences of swimming and diving, I became more attracted to water. It no longer offered the same threat of sleep and death. It was now the life force that had always been present within me. I have become one with it.

In the same way, you can approach your fears using your own creative techniques. It all begins with committing yourself to standing before the fire, before the fear, and using a creative hammer to reshape its disturbing presence. Read your way through it. Paint your way through it. Sing your way through it. But begin the process of seeing it in a new light. Learn about how others have overcome it. Begin to develop new moves to feel more relaxed as it impinges on your desires. Study those who have come before and feel uplifted by their words of wisdom and love.

You are your own blacksmith. You can rework the metal of your being to fashion it anew. In the tradition of Hephaestus, the Greek god of the forge, you can make great things. With your anvil, with your experiences of life, you can forge new steel—you can forge a new direction in life. All that is required is your hammer of resolution and creativeness. Once the fire is started, it would be a shame not to make something with your life.

Striking the Match

A wonderful book to read at this point is *Get Off Your "But"* by Sean Stephenson. It will give you a new perspective on yourself and what you can accomplish. It will help you work through fear and disappointment. It is a really good book to get you off your butt as well.

Find something physical to do if you are not doing something now. Your body needs physical release in order to stay healthy. Your mind also needs the refreshing sense of physical movement. Even a walk on the boardwalk can refresh your mind and body. If there is no boardwalk where you are, seek a large park with trees and grass, so that you can move in nature.

Reflect on what you have read. Consider what fears may be preventing you from getting the most out of life. The beauty of the world is only open to those who can see it. Our time on the planet is limited, so plan to capture wonderful moments through seeing your strengths and your extraordinary power as a creative person.

Connecting to the Hub
Chapter Nine

The wonder of who we are is always wedded to our ability to imagine and to change. We are truly glorious creatures, who have within us the magic of the universe—our consciousness. The ability to lift a pen and write what is on our minds is a gift that is too often ignored. We seek answers but hold back on asking ourselves the questions. We are amazed at Leonardo da Vinci, but we refrain from doing what he did—ask questions, investigate, and keep a journal. He regularly expressed his thoughts on paper, until he discovered new thoughts compounded out of the old thoughts. We expand as we bring new ideas into ourselves, and we grow as we release them. Many of us never release what we have brought into ourselves and so fill up and become congested.

It is in the flow of meaningful conversation, of writing, of painting, or of loving that we allow ourselves the individual expression that keeps us in touch with an ever-changing world. When we do not express our love or creativity, it congeals, and we become sluggish and repetitive. We then vehemently adhere to our personal lies and begin a downward slide, refusing to absorb what we most need: a new story, a new expression of self, an offering of love. All of life requires motion. A rigid tree soon gets broken in strong winds. Our flexibility expands as we are open to the changes that regularly occur around us. The risk of change and the risk of creation keep us alive and functioning at a high level. A new job, a new sculpture, or a new business venture may be filled with anxiety and fear—but it offers a challenge that enlivens the spirit, engages the mind, and brings our creativeness to the forefront of our being.

What are the spokes that need to be acknowledged, strengthened, and nurtured in order for us to fully realize our creative potential? Each of the following qualities provides the support we need to keep our wheels rolling smoothly, without the bumps of an uneven wheel: curiosity, flexibility, self-reliance, persistence, imagination, risk orientation, ability to focus, and openness to new experiences. Anything we want to develop requires dedication, discipline, and openness to new things. Often, as we age, we close down and prevent ourselves from developing new spokes that will help in our later years. No matter what age we are, the willingness to explore can sometimes be suppressed by our fears. We can become more restrictive in our behavior and find ourselves going toward the easy, instead of the more difficult and challenging, where risk is a part of the mix. Some of us have been daring since we were able to walk; others of us have struggled with anything that creates the least bit of anxiety.

Although it would be nice to coast, my suggestion is to find the adventure in you and go for the ring—reach out and attempt something new, something that gives your nerves a tightness, and tests your imagination and self-reliance. When it comes to artistic expression or personal growth, it does not matter how you do in the beginning. What matters is the reaching. What matters are the attempts to explore and re-envision the old and to make new connections in your mind, so that you can create and express in a new way, with freedom and joy. Mankind and womankind have always sought for the sparkle that overcomes the mundane. It is the reason that heroes, stories, and myths have been created through the centuries. You need to go beyond the ordinary, in order to feel vital and creative and to join the present in all its immediacy and wonder.

Our hub is our consciousness, where all experiences, thoughts, and memories come together. It is the controller of the system. It is nurturing and nurtured. We cannot rise above its content, but we can always add to it. When we adamantly adhere to what we have already learned and believed, we prevent a further growth of self. Our beauty and greatness resides in our ability to continually grow and change, regardless of our age. It may be more difficult as we become older, but it is an essential part of keeping us vital and creative. With a hot sun and a lack of water, plants can look downtrodden and depressed. With the blessing of rain, they come alive again and breathe with a new freshness and spirit. In the same way, we can all gain new life and new thoughts by reading and letting the flow of words give birth to a new perspective and new understanding—thereby energizing us and bringing us out of the doldrums. Our hub is important, so that we can keep things turning, but it requires that the spokes are well tended and securely in place. With use, they become loose and worn, leaving room for sudden breakdowns.

Curiosity is one of the spokes that, if worn, can cause us to slip into a lackluster existence, where adventures of the mind become lost and days become well-worn roads filled with dust and regrets. It is important for us to nurture and continue to develop our curiosity, so that we can be as children caught in the wonder of life. The lack of curiosity causes boredom and dead ends in our thinking. Freshness of being and thought come with your curiosity about yourself and the world you live in. Einstein said, "I have no special talents. I am only passionately curious." Who is Shakespeare? Who is that person next to you? Who are you? Questions can lead to answers that are unexpected, have their own twists and turns, and reveal great mysteries and interesting discoveries. Not to wonder about ourselves, other people, and how things happen is to miss one of the great joys of life.

We are spinning in a huge universe. We have developed over one hundred and fifty thousand years. How could we not be curious? Unfortunately, some of us are not curious, or no longer curious. We started out very curious, but with time and school, many have lost that sense of excitement and wonder that gives energy and interest to everyday life. I have had many people come into workshops and classes with the glazed look of ennui and a huge question mark above their heads, asking: What is the next step in my life? Curiosity is always the answer, since it gives you the interest and the energy to find yourself in a new adventure of knowledge or being. We can never tell what is before us. All we can do is be enormously interested in our present moment and how we can use it to help others and ourselves to feel more joyful and fulfilled.

I have always wondered about my own journey through the educational process of formal schooling. At sixteen, I was a high school dropout. At nineteen, I fibbed my way into the New School of Social Research to take courses in creative writing and political science. I was extremely fortunate to have had writing classes with Richard Yates and Hayes B. Jacobs. Richard Yates helped to give me an even stronger interest in writing than I had had, and Hayes B. Jacobs helped me refine my writing, as well as being instrumental in getting me published. If not for him, I would have remained a high school dropout. He suggested that I go back to high school and finish up the two years that I was missing. Although I liked him, and he did play a big part in helping me make the decision to go back to high school, I know that I also decided because I wanted to continue college. Where that desire came from I am not sure.

My father and mother finished the eighth grade. They did not seem upset that they had not completed high school. I am sure they suggested schooling to me. Since it was not a requirement for them, why was it for me? My only thought at this late date is that I was just so curious about things. I also knew that I could not enter college formally until I had finished high school. So, in a burst of energy, while working during the day, I completed two years in one year by going to the Rhodes School in New York City five nights a week, including one summer. It was a private school, and I had to pay for it myself. With the help of lots of scrambled eggs and toast and jelly, I got through it with less trouble than I would have thought. And I liked it.

This enthusiasm for college extended itself into a decision to continue my schooling and go for a master's degree. We are all drawn by different interests. But what is interesting is realizing that some of us think about doing something and then do not do anything to fulfill those yearnings. This is why we have to keep our curiosity at a high level if we are to succeed in manifesting the best of who we are. We must reach inside and uncover our curiosity, even if it has become hidden or thwarted. I was curious about history, about American literature, about psychology, about writing, and about art. I swam in a river of information and knowledge. It provided a way for me to make sense of this strange and wonderful world. We should all become swimmers in our own rivers of interest. In this way, we can gain the confidence that comes from the skills and knowledge that we gain through our chosen endeavors.

For me, it was my curiosity that kept me in school and kept me interested when poverty and divorce tore my life into unhappy chunks. It was curiosity that kept me looking around the next bend in the road to see what new adventures were waiting for me there. However difficult the immediate situations might have been, there was always something new waiting in the wings. It was the way I had learned to see things. To cultivate and expand your curiosity is an essential part of your creativeness and your ability to complete the wheel. You might be able to neglect other things, but curiosity should not be one of them.

Another key to changing circumstances is flexibility. With flexibility, you can notice alternate ways of doing things, alternate strategies. Flexibility maintains your growth and enthusiasm, so that you do not become stuck in futile patterns of response. Unfortunately, if we remain locked in our usual behaviors we open ourselves up to the crushing blows of reality. Sidestepping and reorienting might be a more supportive and imaginative way of dealing with things. Sometimes in relationships, we may find ourselves going through the same motions over and over again, trying to make things right, only to find that we get weaker and weaker and feel deeply disempowered.

The flexibility and curiosity spokes of our wheels need continual care to keep them from causing us uncomfortable bumps and even occasional crashes. Flexibility comes with open-mindedness. It is a practice of suppleness that allows for a suspension of immediate judgment. Sometimes it is difficult to remain objective and open when there are experiences and opinions that disturb us. However, the reward for doing so is greater flexibility and growth. Adherence to a point of view is admirable. But openness to variations is also admirable and instructive. It is better to relax and allow for differences than it is to aggressively resist them and support your inflexibility. There is always time to take a stand after you have allowed the wind to move you. The beauty is in the dance, in the movement of light and color.

To expose your creative nature requires that you pay attention to your most private needs and yearnings. Your intuition will guide you as long as you are open to it. The joy of this path is that you discover who you are, what you most want to do, and how you will proceed during the passing years. Self-reliance springs from the very center of you and provides you with the strength to proceed through the good days and the bad. There will be others who will applaud what you do and support your endeavors. Seek out support, but rely on yourself to inspire your muse, your creativeness, your imaginative spirit. Developing your self-reliance requires that you engage in activities that spark your interests: museums, books, art work, galleries, flea markets, movies, travel on back roads, watching the stars (in the sky, of course), or seeing the ocean gleam in the sunlight. Seek inspiration. Rely on your mind and emotions to respond to your seeking. Let no one dissuade you from your developing creativeness. Your spirit depends on it.

Your hub needs the support of consistently strong spokes. As you look over your experiences, what weaknesses do you see that may have prevented you from achieving the successes you might have wanted? We often pull away from things when we need to pursue them with greater fervor. Persistence is an important aspect to all endeavors. When things do not seem to be going well, our negativity takes over, and we start to convince ourselves that it is not what we want anyway—even if it is the most precious goal that we have had. Since our minds are so good at supporting whatever random negative thoughts we have, we find ourselves arguing for our own defeat. Our lives can present to us many disappointments, but it is important to recognize that succumbing too quickly is not beneficial to our self-esteem or our spirits. Our persistence in spite of the obstacles can lead us to victories that we never imagined. It is a fact that more people have lost what they most wanted as a result of giving up too soon. Developing persistence gives us the necessary time period to make something happen. As I have said to people many times: Sit down in a quiet place and imagine a time in the future, perhaps in five years, when you are without what you most want right now. How does it feel? If you still feel strongly about it, persist now. Do whatever it takes.

When I graduated from the City College of New York with a BA, I decided that I would apply for their master's program. After filling out all the forms and taking the required test, I was fairly certain that I would be accepted into the program. I did not apply at any other college or university, since it seemed to me that with my undergraduate record I would get in. The shock was great when I received their letter of rejection. I kept reading it over and over, trying to understand how this was possible. How could I have been rejected? Well, they must be right. I probably did not get the grades that they were looking for. I should be satisfied with my BA, since I was a high school dropout and had not had much schooling before that. And I am probably not that bright anyway. It is best that I move on with my life and not worry about this one mishap.

However, I did get good grades, and I did have a story published, and I did feel that I could do well in a graduate program. We go through both negative and positive thoughts to reconcile what has happened to us. We fight within ourselves with the "I'm not worthy" syndrome over and over again, until we decide to pull away from what hurts us. Just because it hurts does not mean you need to succumb to fleeing the pain.

Late one night, with all the wrestling that my conscience could stand, I decided I would ask for an interview with the dean of the college. I realized that I would only have this one chance to change my situation. It was a bold move, and I had not done bold moves like this before, but I recognized that this was something that I really wanted and that to give up by accepting an impersonal letter of rejection did not make sense. I struggled with my anxiety for over a week, before I received notice that the dean would meet with me.

When I went into his office, I felt nervous and uncomfortable. It was such a formal-looking office with its books, diplomas, certificates, and awards. I felt impressed and overwhelmed. Out of a box that I had brought with me, I pulled all the papers I had written for the different classes I had taken at the college, including the story that had just been published, and I laid them on his desk. They came to a height of about a foot and a half. I remember feeling very good about the height of the stack. He listened to me and said at different points during my plea that these decisions were not made lightly and that he did not know how this situation could be altered. He began going through the stack, pulling essays from different places in the stack.

Although there were many As and Bs, as well as some Cs, I did not have them stacked with all the A papers on top. I had spread them throughout the stack. The dean looked over a number of essays from different parts of the stack. However, he pulled out one essay that he read almost all the way through. It was an essay concerning Joseph Conrad's novel in which I talked about potash and Conrad and the wonder of beautifully blown glass. After finishing the essay, he made a decision. I am not sure if it was the stack of papers, what I had said to him, or the Conrad essay that convinced him, but he accepted me into the program—to my great surprise and joy! It was a monumental event and one that I would not have wanted to miss in this life. If I had not persisted against the odds, I would never have received my master's in English some years later. Persistence is an important trait to develop. Your wheel's balance depends upon it.

So often in this age of computers, the Internet, TV, and music videos, we allow our imaginations to lie fallow in some dark field of our minds. Its multicolored flowers and evergreen branches are no longer inspiring us to playfully wander through our drifting reveries and daydreams. We are given to obsessive contacts that distort our time and control our behavior. We view the world through electronically controlled windows, distant and glass enclosed. We are trapped by our recently constructed mythology that connection is of primary importance. Privacy is a word that is quickly losing all meaning. Imagination is a word that needs to be taught in college, since so many people have lost its power in their confrontation with the "online" generation. Even our monsters are previsualized for us. How often do we privately engage in using our imaginations to visualize and form adventures that transcend the mundane repetition of predictable shows? How do we nurture our creativity when we are bombarded by technologically aggressive experiences of reality? Can we find ourselves beyond reality TV? Or are we so convinced that continual contact with this altered world view is our true function? Unfortunately, our creativity dies between blaring commercials. Are not the beauty and wonder of our own beings more in need of us than this passing wizardry?

Our imaginations can form a world that is uniquely ours and not a mirror of the consumer one, where constipation and pimples are ongoing problems. To cultivate our imaginations, we need to use them. We need to bring them out of the dusty closet with the old clothes and toys that have lost their vitality and wholeness. Old toys are rich in mystery. As we view them, we see a lost wheel here, a missing eye there, and a part that has no place to go. We could say they are junk, and we don't need them—but on some deep kid level we know we need them. Perhaps is it the part that has no immediate reference that can help ancient jungles of our minds. We could explore with Tarzan sequestered areas of jungle that contain significant clues for solving the mystery. As we now swing from the vines of our imaginations, we will regain our creative sparks that set all things in motion.

Exercising our imaginations is an important aspect of our life experiences. A handsome older woman, with long silver and black hair that was swept back in an untidy and girlish-looking bun, sat across from us in my writing workshop. She read her personal story in a slow but controlled voice that had a sweet sensuality to it. As she read the story, we were intrigued by the uncertainty of it. The summer heat and the sounds of the cicadas gave a strange backdrop to the meal she had made for her new male guest. Everything was described in such infinite detail that you wondered when his hand touched her shoulder where it would lead. Everything was so matter of fact that the current movement of the story seemed out of character. Before our quiet and expectant faces, she slowly described her sexual experience with this new acquaintance. The beauty of the story would be difficult to describe, but the revelation of the experience was beyond what any of us had expected in our writing group. She then told us that she was going blind, and that the group had given her the courage to explore her thoughts and her feelings. She told us that, since she was lonely, she wanted to have one more sexual experience before she became totally blind. She also wanted to share it with the group, so that they could see how valuable they had been to her. Each of us is bound to the other. We all share this wonderful adventure called life. It is through our imagination and storytelling that we can share our experiences and our creativeness. We are filled with stories that need telling, so that we can feel for each other as well as unburden ourselves. The telling of stories around the fire was cathartic. It was a sharing of the most profound sense of who we are.

This extraordinary woman took a risk to share her feelings and her thoughts with the group. If we are to meet the challenge of life, then each of us must risk. If we are to grow and to exceed what we have done before, we must risk. Through testing ourselves, we strengthen our ability. The stronger we get, the easier it is for us to express our deepest feelings with honesty and courage. Through this woman's willingness to go beyond the ordinary and courageously express her deepest feelings, all of us were led out of the comfort of our contained existence. In the following meetings, more and more of the individual members expressed themselves with courage and directness. This single spark that ignited the fire gave voice to us all. We must not hold back. Strike that match, and join in the warmth of a shared fire.

The beauty of a story comes from the focus of the author. Although the story may unfold with its own energy, it still requires a holding together through the author's ability to focus and remain aware of its movement. The key in all of our endeavors is focus. If we lose focus, we begin to drift from our assigned course and we may lose our way. To make sure our wheel is balanced, we need to regularly check our focus and the strength and evenness of the spokes that are joined to our hub. To keep things running smoothly, we cannot lose our focus.

To explore our creativity, we must be open to new experiences. We must allow our imaginations to flourish and take flight. They must not be controlled by fear or doubt or the overwhelming preponderance of technology. It is important that we cultivate our curiosity, so that we can energize our muses and inspire creative expressions. We expand ourselves and our creativity by being flexible and persistent. When we close down, we lose the flow, and we begin to worry about the meaning of our expressions. As long as you stay focused, you will uncover your deepest ideas and feelings. Through trusting your intuition, you will find within the strength to be self-reliant and willing to live with the ambiguity and uncertainty that life presents to us as we explore the depths. No journey is without its risks. However, it is in confronting the risks and uncertainties that we are able to realize ourselves and our fondest dreams. This journey that we have entered into is one that provides the most fulfilling outcomes, because it brings to the surface what is most true about us.

Our hub contains all our experiences, thoughts, and feelings. Our strength lies in our ability to share and to mold these into something of beauty. It does not matter what shape or form it takes, as long as it represents your insight, your love, and your individuality. You can express it as a philosophy, a painting, a story, a sketch, a journal, or anything that you can give honest and sincere expression to. Your carefully constructed spokes will help you to overcome any obstacles to your self-expression and creativeness. The strength of your wheel will guide you through the rough roads. I believe I see a rainbow. I hope you can too.

Impressions of a seacoast

Striking the Match

Write down two goals that stretch you, that make you quiver with excitement. Set a time period for accomplishing them, and get started on your new course of action. They do not have to be earth shattering, but they do need to make you feel stronger after you complete them.

Goals are about staying focused and persistence. It is good to regularly set new goals to keep yourself on track. Often we let things just happen to us. Goals allow us to go for those things that we want. Goals can be moral, educational, physical, spiritual, or health oriented. They could also be about giving more hugs, buying flowers for your special person, or spending more time playing games with your children. Goals give you a way to enjoy more of your life.

Although we all know that meditation is probably good for our nervous system and our heart, we seem to rarely expose ourselves to its relaxing benefits. I suggest you begin now by taking fifteen minutes of your day to calmly think of nothing. Allow yourself the possibility of discovering the reason for meditation's endurance through the centuries.

Imaginative Freedom
Chapter Ten

If I am not for myself,
Then who can be for me?
But if I am only for myself,
Then who am I?
And if not now, when?
—Hillel

Time is a pressing factor in the lives of all of us. Our freedom is limited to the time we have, so it is important that we use it well. We complain that we do not have enough time to do all that we would like to do, but what do we have to do? Finding our paths and unearthing our treasures is to me the wonder of wonders. It is not easy to use time well. Whether we are young or old, finding what moves us and engages our attention is what will bring us the most joy. It is not so much what we do, as how we do it, and how much satisfaction it gives us. Tending a garden in the early morning, when dampness is still present and the smell of earth captures our attention, can give us a feeling of completeness and love that a high-in-the-sky office might not. To attain freedom, we must uncover and discard the chains that bind us. It is what our art is for: to free us from the restrictions of thoughts, fears, and hesitations and to lift us from the mundane to a vision of beauty and joy.

In our search for recognition and financial success, many of us lose our ability to appreciate our life experience. We are often devoid of the devotion and excitement that should be part of our daily lives. I think about the wonderful excitement a child has when he or she sees his father or mother after a long day's absence. The development of our creativeness can help us to re-experience that kind of excitement. We are unique, and our uniqueness, which includes who we are and how we think, is a resource that needs to be shared with others. As we develop our skills, we should seek to share them with others, so that the enthusiasm and joy of their expression can spread. We have created art throughout the centuries. It gives our minds, our souls, and our mythology an expression that unifies us and tells our stories. In the drawing of a line, the writing of a word, and the playing of music, we touch the soul of who we are. Each of us needs that connection, so that, like the child within us, we can feel the excitement and exuberance that is our heritage.

Completing the wheel is an undertaking that can be exasperating, fearful, and annoying—as well as wonderful, exhilarating, and joyful. As we have seen, the journey is one that requires honesty, strength, and a desire to uncover the deepest part of ourselves. Each of us longs for some realization about the meaning of life and the ability to tell our own story. It is this that binds us together and can give us our freedom. So often we restrict ourselves by thoughts that conflict with our imaginative freedom and confine us to battling with whether we can do something creative or not. Thoughts that limit our freedom usually come from a place of fear, uncertainty, and lagging self-esteem. To change this scenario, you need to engage in the thick of your negativity and your imagined lack of freedom. What you think is your secret. You can call people outrageous names and they will never know. You have always been free to think what you will.

However, just like everything else that you want to get good at, you have to practice. Your mind gets looser the more you play with it. Your imagination gets freer the more you play with it. To keep thinking the same restrictive thoughts will only perpetuate what you have always thought. *I need someone to stand over me and force me to write. I am too lazy to do anything on a regular basis. It is so much easier for some people than it is for others. It has always been hard for me.* There are always thoughts that can weaken you and deny you the freedom that you really possess. There may be a few people who do not need to do much to make things happen. However, I just have not met them. In my experience, most people require disciplined action to achieve what they want in their lives. To come up with new thoughts and actions, you must think, read, and do. Imaginative freedom comes from overcoming the thoughts that bind you and playfully engaging the wilderness of your mind.

We have the unique capacity to rearrange and extrapolate from material that we have stored in different corners of our minds. How we do that is still a mystery, but what isn't is our power to reorganize and create something new from this storehouse. Our imaginative freedom has developed past civilizations and our current world's societies.

Developing your thinking and your imagination is key to gaining a profound freedom within yourself. Death is not the enemy. Failure of vision is the enemy. When you feel stopped, blocked, or overwhelmed, bathe yourself in imagery. Go to the movies, go to museums, go to art galleries, watch documentaries, take a long drive and absorb the scenery, take pictures—anything that will overload your mind with new visual content. From this potpourri you will be able to free yourself from restrictive thoughts and blocks. One tiny image or a part of an image can set your mind onto a whole new path. Words can ignite your spirit and send you in a more fulfilling direction that contains meaning and purpose.

Throughout the years there have been two images, by two different artists, that I have held onto with fervor. They have been with me through seven different homes, six cities, and two different states, New York and Florida. They have been rolled and unrolled; they have spent time unframed and then framed. They have always been there with me as a kind of symbolic token of something deep within me that I have been exploring in recent years. It is interesting to discover the things that we value. They usually hold more significance than we realize, as we transport them from place to place. What do you have that you have carried from place to place, that has particular meaning to you, that you have not appreciated? As I was rehanging my tokens a few years ago, I reviewed the stories that go along with the images.

One of them, now framed, is a poster by Christo called *Paris Review 1982*. I discovered it in a little art store in East Hampton that my girlfriend had decided to browse through. I am always a little surprised when certain unexpected things happen, and then years later the significance of them becomes clear. I would never have gone into this place myself. It is always good to take advantage of spontaneous situations that might hold something significant. I always ask, "What is here that I have come for?" If, as I walk about, nothing speaks to me, at least I know I tried to get the most out of the visit. However, there are times when this accidental meeting with place or person proves insightful. I know this particular poster was waiting for me, since as soon as I flipped to it, I found it so attractive and interesting. I was not sure what it was about the poster, except that I had to get it. When you are moved by something, take action. Do not let it slip away.

As I reviewed this poster on the wall in its shiny new frame, I realized that it speaks of my youth, that it symbolizes my early love of writing and art. I suddenly remembered buying copies of the *Paris Review* from the bursting newsstands on Broadway in New York City. They always had magazines and newspapers from all over the world, which were stacked in every bit of space the wooden shack could provide. It always gave me a sense that there was a lot happening in the world. But the *Paris Review* gave me wonderful visual sensations of Paris, of the ex-patriots, of Hemingway, of wine, of cobbled streets, and the Shakespeare and Company bookstore. As a young man, I desired to travel the streets of Paris and meet infamous authors. But marriage and money limited my wanderings to the Bronx. So perhaps in the beginning it represented my fantasy life.

I have tacked it to different walls with white pushpins. I have carefully rolled it many times, as I have left one place for another, each time hoping it would be the last one. Finally, I bought a wide gold metal frame, complete with glass, to more permanently display this traveling work of art. As I have stared at it, wondering what my fascination with it is, I have seen that I am also tied. I am tied within myself, preventing myself from expressing and doing, held back by forces that lie hidden. However I struggle with it, as in the image, I am always bound by this invisible twine. Yet it is such a restful image, resolute and patient, with a touch of mystery. Perhaps it is the mystery of it that has held my interest all these years. What is within the bound pages of the magazine that I might want to know? Perhaps some secret could be revealed within its pages that could alter my life. When something is covered, there is always that tempting wish to have it uncovered and exposed—the seventh veil, as it were. However, there is something intrinsically interesting in things wrapped. A gift, a surprise, a puzzle—they all hold our attention, and in the passing years maybe I have been captivated by all of them. There is a part of me that remains hidden and under wraps. Part of the process of writing is to slowly uncover the deeper parts of ourselves, so that we can be free of their holding power. The joy then is in uncovering, as an archeologist seeking a new artifact to further develop a theory about what lies beneath.

Although I have come to no conclusions about the poster, I find it engaging to discover what motives or attractions were part of the selection and retention of the image. It gives me a thread on which to build, a connection that might reveal to me something that I have been looking for over the years. As we find ourselves, we find others. We discover those essential human concerns and emotions that help us to communicate. What is also interesting is that I bought this poster because at least ten years earlier I had *not* bought a painting that I had liked very much. As a result, I ended up thinking about it at different times over the years, complaining that I had not bought it. I told myself I would never do that again.

Christo's poster gave me a sense of Art. As I developed my skills as a photographer, I would always wonder how artistic my photographs were. Did I capture something in a way that was truly interesting and revealing, or was it mundane and usual? Christo's *Paris Review 1982* gave me a strong sense of the creative and innovative. It helped me to evaluate where I was and how I was doing. It may seem strange, but even though it had nothing to do with my own images, it gave me an idea of the level of art that I was reaching for. Its simplicity helped me to see the profound. Each of us contributes to the other, as long as we allow ourselves to be open to what is presented, either accidentally or forthrightly. I was blessed with this poster.

I was also blessed by the painting that I did not buy. It became an image in my mind that lingered through the years and gave me a strong sense of how important it is to act when you feel drawn to something. I saw the painting during a wonderful vacation in Maine. My ex-wife and I decided to spend part of our vacation in Bar Harbor to see Arcadia National Park and McKay's Public House, a delightful restaurant that had very good food and wonderful antiques. During our five-day stay at this location, we delighted in camping for two days in the park and three at a utility rental that was lovely, since it was damp-free and warm at night. On a Saturday or Sunday afternoon there was a street fair that brought all the visitors to walk Main Street to see what wonders might be gotten in the delightfully quaint town. My ex-wife had decided that this was a perfect excursion for us. I reluctantly followed, with doubt on my face and leaden feet. It is possible that I complained about the stopping and going and viewing and moving. I was less patient back then. I remember a tall standing clock along Main Street and somewhat staring at its large hands, perhaps waiting for time to pass. However, I did begin to walk through outdoor and indoor exhibits. I became captivated by the art. The items were so very different from anything I had seen before. In a few of the paintings there were beautiful beach pebbles and rocks that contained their natural grain, so that you almost felt you could touch them if they just fell off the canvas. And then there were the white spaces of the canvases, as if the paintings were not finished as yet. But the white space brought the view so powerfully before your eyes that you were grateful for its ability to bring you into the pebbles and stones; it provided you with a sense of beauty that you would ordinarily miss. It was an experience just to see the paintings of Alan Magee. I wanted so much to have one of these paintings, but our budgeted vacation only allowed for so many extras and my ex-wife did not particularly like the paintings. Unfortunately, I struggled in my mind for a while and then let the painting go.

This painting stayed locked within my memory over the years, until I accidentally rediscovered Alan Magee and his painting *Constellation*. I was in Woodstock, New York, with a photography group that I was teaching, and I decided to go into a bookstore that I particularly liked. As I wondered around, having gained that skill to be open to something that was waiting for me, I saw a postcard holder that had some interesting and unusual cards in it. As I turned the wheel, I saw one of Alan Magee's paintings. I could not believe it. I was so excited to find this image after so many years. It had to be at least fifteen years, and I didn't even know his name until I saw it on the back of the card.

This card image has been with me now for about ten years, but the original images have been with me for over thirty years. The question is: What is it that has had such a powerful impact on my mind and left such an indelible impression? As I view the card, I feel a sense of peace. There is a quietness about the stones, with their muted colors and strategic placements. Unlike the natural world, it has human order to it. It resonates of a higher intelligence. There is no dirt between the stones and pebbles to disrupt the individual beauty that they have. They remain pristine, with their shifting lines and dots, their rough plainness and smooth coolness. All are unique within their varying shapes and colors, jewels to charm and delight any collector. So where is the answer to the puzzle of transcending time and place? What has moved me to this state of attachment? I believe it is the beauty of it all.

To develop your creativeness is to develop your ability to see and feel beauty on a level that is more meaningful and inspiring than the usual experience. It is the understanding and the presence of beauty that arrests our aggressive and fearful hearts. We each can gain our own sense of beauty, as we reflect on the things that emotionally move us, that capture our attention and passion. Our brains respond to beauty with an excitement that brings about enjoyment and love. It gives us a way to enrich ourselves and enrich others by the sharing of our creative expressions. Beauty moves us to go beyond ourselves, whether it is in the brush strokes of a calligrapher or the soft kisses of a lover's embrace. The good life is the life that contains expressions of beauty deeply felt and understood by the participant. I have come to see that I have traveled with these two works of art, *Constellations* and *Paris Review 1982*, because they have given me a sense of the beauty that I seek in my own creative expressions.

Some years ago, I decided that I wanted to photograph nudes. Aside from the fact that I always thought a woman's body was truly beautiful, there was something in the long tradition of nudes and the drawing of nudes that became fascinating to me. The power of birth resides within the curved body of a woman. How does one capture that in a drawing or a photograph? The grace of gestures and movements are so wonderfully expressed in women. How do you capture a woman's beauty in an image? As you attempt to draw a woman, or photograph her, you learn about lines and curves, about light and shadow, about expression and desire. As you confront her skin, you confront your own skin and the wonder that it contains. As you see the beauty in another, you see the beauty within yourself. We yearn for many things in life, but to confront the beauty of a moment and record it gives us sublime pleasure.

There are two images from photographing nudes that now follow me wherever I go. One was taken during a workshop in Woodstock. It was a warm day, and the morning sun peeked through tall trees and sudden openings of land. The young women were from a local college and they were somewhat nervous, though prepared to model naked in the shelter of the woods. Although there was a small group of photographers and specific assignments, I wanted only to capture spontaneously and not through tedious direction. As the day moved toward afternoon, one of the women, Rebecca, went into the open porch of a shack that had been built just above a slow-moving stream, where all the others were being photographed. In the subdued light that drifted through the dusty windows and old, rusty-looking screens, Rebecca put her hand up against a window frame and relaxed. She seemed transported for the moment into a reverie that placed her beyond the current synthetic situation. Her nudity was forgotten, and she wandered through her private thoughts without the consciousness of her surroundings. There was such beauty in that moment as I viewed her. Her body was relaxed and her mind caught up in a thousand thoughts. In that brief moment, I photographed her. In that brief moment, I loved her. I cherish the photograph for the sacredness of the moment, for the beauty of Rebecca, and for the acceptance of the exchange.

The second image was taken in Florida, at a workshop that Robert Farber gave. We were on the lush grounds of a beautiful home that was tucked away between the romantic folds of palm trees, foliage, stone walkways, and a distinct trickling stream. It was a place of magic. The image that I selected from that shoot was one that represented our eternal attachment to nature and all the wonders that derive from its existence. There is an extraordinary entwining of nature and women in this photograph, which expresses the total reliance we have on both for our survival. Beauty is always before us. The creativity of nature is within us. It is up to us to express it.

Imaginative freedom comes from discipline and from being aware. It comes from developing the skill to recognize with the passing moments when the time is right, or the challenge is right, or the coincidence is right. Only you can decide. However, all the "Striking the Match" invitations should bring you to a point of being ready. Each should bring you closer to who you are and what you need to express, so that your joy and your life can be given the imaginative freedom they deserve. There are no easy answers to the questions of life. We are beautifully caught on a spinning planet that offers sunlight and rain. In all its richness we reside for a time. Applaud your uniqueness; applaud your time here, so that others can feel your presence and perhaps feel comforted by your artifacts—even if it is just your children or friends who will treasure them.

Completing the wheel is about balancing yourself, about bringing your life into a focus, so that you can feel the joy of your own individual love and creativeness. When you are out of balance, you wobble. Your path becomes bumpy and rut-filled. By knowing your power and your skills, you are able to overcome any impediments that might confront you. If you are not sure of what you want to do, doodle. Somewhere within the doodle is your answer. We often hold ourselves back by our unwillingness to confront ourselves. Since you have done the exercises in this book, as so many others have in the past, you will have strengthened who you are and what you want—more than you would have thought possible at the beginning of this journey.

I wish for you beauty and imaginative freedom.